MIND-BENDING

Also by Lowell D. Streiker

The Gospel Time Bomb
Cults: The Continuing Threat
The Cults Are Coming!
The Jesus Trip: Advent of the Jesus Freaks
Religion and the New Majority: Billy Graham, Middle America, and the Politics of the 70s (with Gerald S. Strober)
The Gospel of Irreligious Religion
Who Am I? Second Thoughts on Man, His Loves, His Gods
The Promise of Buber

MIND-BENDING

Brainwashing, Cults, and Deprogramming in the '80s

Lowell D. Streiker

DOUBLEDAY & COMPANY, INC.

GARDEN CITY, NEW YORK

1984

Library of Congress Cataloging in Publication Data
Streiker, Lowell D.
    Mind-bending: brainwashing, cults, and deprogramming
    in the '80s.
    1. Cults.   2. Sects.   3. Deprogramming.   I. Title.
BP603.S84   1984   291
    ISBN: 0-385-19275-4
    Library of Congress Catalog Card Number: 83–25393

To Miss T., Charles, TEB and ML, Ralph
and Jean

ACKNOWLEDGMENTS

The author wishes to thank Eva Maiden and Zev Putterman for reading the manuscript and offering many helpful suggestions. He also wishes to express his gratitude to Aggie and Baggie (Agnes Stogdell and Betty Johnson) for assisting in the reading of the proofs.

Preface

"Mind-bending" is a slang term for experiences which strongly influence the mind. It is the word which I have chosen to describe a cluster of processes through which cults, sects, and other agents of persuasive influence throw their potential converts off balance emotionally, induce cathartic reactions, and produce in them radically altered attitudes and new patterns of behavior. Such sudden changes in beliefs and actions have been described by others as "snapping," and have been accounted for as the results of "brainwashing." According to the proponents of the snapping/brainwashing hypothesis, the convert no longer exercises freedom of will. The individual has lost control, has been reduced to the status of a puppet. Critics of cult conversion often maintain that the recruit has been hypnotized, i.e., that he has fallen under the spell of another person, and that he has no choice but to obey.

I have chosen to call the processes through which individuals are influenced "mind-bending" because I recognize that one's perception of reality, values, and self-image are definitely "bent" or distorted by these techniques. However, I reject the notion that there exists a "technology of mind control" through which artful and designing persons are able to rob us of our freedom. Autonomy is often given away, but it is seldom stolen. It is my contention that we freely choose to be influenced, choose to conspire with others to relinquish control to them, choose to shirk responsibility, and choose to negligently allow automatic and unconscious processes within ourselves to rule us.

Even in the most extreme forms of mind manipulation—e.g., if someone were to administer a psychedelic drug to a subject without the subject's knowledge—the outcome depends as much on what the subject brings to the experience as it does on what the mind-blowing agent causes. A mind can only be bent according to its bent. The outcome of mind-bending depends upon the receptivity of the subject and the persistence of the mind-bender.

There are processes which distort our perception, subtly incline us to conform to groups and obey authority figures, encourage our dependencies, and incline us to reject personal responsibility and to allow others to program our behavior, attitudes, and beliefs. As we shall see, they are not mysterious, occult, or irresistible. But neither are they ineffective. These processes can be used by us for ourselves or by others against our best interests. We can protect ourselves against them, counteract their effects, and heal ourselves of the harm which they occasionally cause.

Mind-bending is real and has great potential for evil as well as for good. However, it is not brainwashing, mind control, hypnosis; nor does it cause mental illness, permanent harm to the central nervous system, psychosis, or a predisposition to murder or suicide.

Mind-bending is a book about freedom and the future of America. It is about being born again, charisma, child abuse, conformity, conversion, decision making, the family, healing, law and order, morality, religion, and ultrafundamentalism. Basically, this is a book about influence (proper and undue), distorting the truth, and fanaticism. Some of the fanatics cited are members of cults and sects and some are deprogrammers —which leads me to how I learned about mind-bending in the first place.

For five years I have served as director of Freedom Counseling Center, a professional service which helps individuals and families whose lives have been disturbed by cults, sects, and various other authoritarian groups. *Mind-bending* is, in part, an account of my career as a counselor of individuals and families who have been affected by cults, a career which began with my involvement with the mayhem of the People's Temple and which continues today—two thousand cases later. It is a statement of my "moderate" position on the issues of "deprogramming," "conversion," "deconversion," the "rehabilitation" of former cultists, and the mediating of cult-related family struggles. It is an examination of what cults really are and what they tell us about ourselves and our future.

The word "cult" has become a call to battle, the trumpet signaling a struggle of the gravest significance. Empowered by the "negative metaphor" of Jonestown, relatives of cult members are successfully lobbying for legislation which essentially makes conversion to a nontraditional religion evidence of mental illness and the basis for the suspension of the convert's civil rights. As we shall detail, the flimsiest connection with anything which by the remotest coincidence can be associated with "cults" or described as "mind control" has become the basis for extralegal acts of intervention which until a decade ago were virtually foreign to our society and its mores. Without exaggeration, critics of "the great cult scare" have warned that not only are the fates of a handful of troublesome new religions at stake but also "the shape of religious freedom and civil liberties in the future."[1]

What is a cult? Is the term useful or has it died of careless overapplication? Does the word have any utility or should it be stricken from the language? What exactly does the word "cult" mean? The most common definitions (with their sources given in parentheses) are "the veneration of a deity . . . excessive or fanatic devotion" (the dictionary); "a belief system which deviates from the evangelical Christian interpretation of the Bible" (a Baptist minister); "destructive, avaricious groups which employ brainwashing techniques to transform their victims into mindless robots and zombies" (a deprogrammer); "a pejorative term for a religion other than one's own, a term of opprobrium like 'nigger' " (a Unification Church spokesman); "any new or syncretistic religious movement" (a historian); "a term popularly and incorrectly applied to a wide variety of religious sects, communal groups, meditation societies, and psychological therapies" (a sociologist).

Since Jonestown, "cult" usually connotes nothing good.

Whatever the word means (and we shall explain possible definitions further), it should be recognized that cults are movements of personal affirmation and social protest. They give expression to basic feelings: "There is something wrong with this society" and "there is something wrong with me." But cults do not merely give vent to frustrations. Cults say that something can be done: the convert can be *somebody* and with the help of the group he can remake the world.

Believing that the individual can be perfected and that he or she can *make a difference* in the social arena is a distinctively American way of perceiving reality. More than two centuries of voluntarism and social reform have been inspired by just such convictions. Cults are more American than their critics suspect. They are microcosms of the greater society, weather vanes supersensitive to winds of change. Cults are idealistic expressions of the freedom to seek, find, and believe which Americans cherish. They are also "the lunatic fringe," the virulent cells growing out of control which may prove malignant or benign or even a valued new mutation. As for the menace of cults, imagine anything which you consider vile, disgusting, dishonest, harmful, or revolting, and I can guarantee that some group with which I have dealt during the past five years has routinely countenanced that act "in the name of God"!

Cults may be unusual and irksome but they are not alien. They are manifestations of what is happening to America as a civilization at this time in our history. For the cult controversy illumines not only conflicts of generation and values but shifts in perception about the way the world is, the way it will be, and what ought to be done about both.

NOTE

In these pages, I have told the truth as clearly, as comprehensively, and as accurately as I could remember it. Occasionally I have changed names or circumstantial details in order to maintain pledges of confidentiality or because it was my opinion or the opinion of my publisher that anonymity was proper and desirable.

Contents

MIND-BENDING

1

Beginnings

CONVERSION CONFUSIONS

I might as well start at the beginning. But which beginning? There have been several.

One beginning was my conversion to Christianity, which occurred when I was fifteen years old. It was the beginning of my immersion in and preoccupation with religion. If I had not "gone forward" at a Chicagoland Youth for Christ rally to "accept Jesus" as my "personal savior," I would probably have missed out on a wealth of firsthand experience, would have developed radically different friendships and career goals, and, most assuredly, would not have spent a quarter of a century exploring the frontiers between so-called normal society and fringe religiosity.

Further, had I not begun my junior year at Austin High School as one who had dedicated his life to the "lordship of Jesus Christ," I would not have caused such grave concern, disappointment, and anxiety to my concerned relatives and friends. It is sad to say, but my having been the object of the desperate efforts of my loved ones—my having responded as well as I could to their heartbreak—has proved the secret ingredient in the recipe of training, life experience, deliberate choices, and accidents which have made me the person I am today.

MOODY BIBLE INSTITUTE

Another beginning was my short tenure as an editor at Moody Bible Institute in Chicago. While preparing issues of "Moody Memo," the house organ of the "West Point of Christian service," I met two high-spirited mavericks who valued my intelligence and humor and would not allow me to use my evangelical faith as a place of refuge from the demands which abilities place upon a young man. The first was Elizabeth A. Thompson, "Miss T.," my boss in the editorial division of Moody Press. Miss T. was sixty-eight years old, a tiny sprite of a woman with yellow-white hair and a most emphatic manner of speech and movement. She had been with Moody Press and its predecessor organization (the Bible Institute Colportage Association) for fifty years when our friendship began. The other maverick was Charles F. Pfeiffer, Moody's Old Testament professor, who was expert in Egyptology, Assyriology, the Dead Sea Scrolls, scores of languages both ancient and modern, and more additional areas than I can remember. Pfeiffer was about forty then—already totally bald and with a complete set of false teeth. He seemingly never slept, could be found in his small office with its thousands of books at almost any hour of the day or night.

When I went to work at MBI, I was eighteen, married, and had completed one year of college. Miss T. wanted me to return to college. She was an honest, righteous Scottish spinster who had managed so long on a diet of self-denial that she wanted very little. She had avoided marriage in order to care for an invalid mother who had lived until ninety-five and who left her daughter with thousands of dollars in unpaid hospital bills. Miss T. also wanted to impart to me her values of hard work, honesty, and openness to growth. She also taught me the difference between piety and pious nonsense.

Charley wanted me to be a scholar like himself—preferably a master of Hebrew and cognate languages. After all, he reasoned, I was a "Hebrew Christian." So the Old Testament was much more my heritage than it was his. After a futile attempt to teach me Arabic, he encouraged me to learn Greek (which was much more to my liking) and finally helped arrange a scholarship opportunity for me at his alma mater, Temple University in Philadelphia. He hoped that I would continue on to Dropsie College of Hebrew and Cognate Learning, where he had earned his doctorate, but he was in no way disappointed when I chose Princeton University.

"THE CULTS ARE COMING!"—A PREMONITION

The beginning which is the most relevant to this book was in July 1978. At the time, I was executive director of the Mental Health Association of San Mateo County, California. My office was in the city of San Mateo, which is about twenty miles south of San Francisco. A few months earlier, my book *The Cults Are Coming!* had been published. That book, in turn, had been prompted by my longtime fascination with contemporary religious movements, by a personal experience with the most publicized of the new groups—the conversion and subsequent defection of a dear friend from the Unification Church of Sun Myung Moon—and by the persistent urgings of my wife, who kept reporting her "gut feeling" that "cults are going to be important soon."

The appearance of the book occasioned a trickle of phone calls from anguished parents whose offspring had found their way into groups such as those mentioned in *The Cults Are Coming!* (the Moonies, the Children of God, and the Hare Krishnas) as well as some nastier sects then unfamiliar to me. Since I was not an active interventionist but only a sympathetic observer of the cult phenomenon and of parental reactions, there was nothing I could do but listen, provide general advice, and recommend a book or two.

Then Claire Bouquet phoned. Her son Brian, she related, was in a place called Jonestown in Guyana, South America. Jonestown, she said, was the enclave of the People's Temple, a northern California sect headed by a healer-evangelist named Jim Jones. Jones had received enough media attention for me to be familiar with his name and questionable reputation. As I worked on the manuscript to my book, defectors from the People's Temple were spreading tales of beatings, threats, theft of property, sexual improprieties, and worse. The regularly scheduled radio broadcasts of Jones's sermons and healings services had mysteriously been suspended even though display ads still ran in both San Francisco daily newspapers. Telephone calls to the Temple were unanswered. My original outline for *The Cults Are Coming!* had included a section on the People's Temple, but my editor had asked me to delete it because his publication committee felt that the People's Temple and Jim Jones were purely California phenomena of little possible interest to anyone but Californians!

But many years of participative observation of extremist sects and the scare headlines about Jones prepared me little for Claire Bouquet. She was animated, articulate, and overpowering. She wove together a tapestry of gloom and doom from defectors' accusations, a mother's intuition, inferential surmises, yellow-journalistic speculations, and awful, terrifying forebodings. She detailed her frustrating conversations with government officials, a radiotelephone conversation with Brian through which she "knew" he was trying to tell her that things were not right at the utopian experiment in the jungle, her appeals to the media, including the tabloids, and even her efforts to recruit a Rhodesian mercenary to undertake an armed rescue of her son. It was this last detail which put me off. I became convinced that Claire was a crackpot, like the Kennedy assassination theorists I had interviewed when I co-produced and moderated a public service talk show for the CBS flagship station, WCAU-TV (Philadelphia), or like the evangelist's wife (a high school chum's mother) who told me in a solemn conspiratorial manner of a man she knew who was being persecuted by the AMA and the American Cancer Society because he had discovered a cure for cancer and, of course, all those rich doctors could not permit him to destroy their livelihood.

And so poor Claire and the whole Jonestown mess was filed away in the recesses of my mind for future reference. Until

Joan Culpepper called. Joan seemed even more bizarre than Claire. She was a fast-talking Los Angelino who had the habit of name-dropping, claiming that her movie-star and rock-and-roll-luminary friends would lend their support to her new effort. In an accent which seemed to me part LA and part Bakersfield, Joan told me of her background in advertising, show business, and as a follower of "Bo and Peep" in an obscure UFO cult. She identified herself as an officer of a fledgling anticult organization called "the Human Freedom Center" with branches in Berkeley and Encino near LA. The group had dual purposes: creating public awareness of and "legal" remedies for "mental kidnapping" and other cult nastiness, and providing shelter and refuge to escapees from Jonestown (which the Human Freedom Center expected to collapse momentarily as the result of the machinations of an HFC affiliate, the Concerned Relatives). I found much of Joan's rhetoric distasteful—and told her so. I wanted then and I want today no laws against "mental kidnapping" or "mentacide" or any other socially unacceptable state of mind. Yet there was something innately warm and human about Joan that enabled us to interact and continue our telephone discussion despite my objections to the models by which she expressed herself.

Joan stated that she was about to come north for a meeting of the HFC board of directors to be held that coming Sunday at the Berkeley location. She invited me to attend and to consider becoming a consultant or adviser. She flattered me a bit, declaring that not only was my knowledge of cults valuable to HFC but my experience as the director of a nonprofit, charitable agency would also be helpful. Perhaps, she remarked, I would be interested in sharing with the amateurs who had founded HFC my organizational, fund-raising, and public relations expertise. I accepted her invitation and, in a few days, my wife and I made the one-hour drive across San Francisco Bay from our home in Foster City to the large old house on Regent Street next to Alta Bates Hospital.

My initial impressions were mixed and confused. The building was a sparsely furnished, down-at-the-heels nursing home with ratty, abused sofas and armchairs, much evidence of negligent maintenance (a broken molding in the living room, a missing lock in the guest bathroom, fading and peeling paint throughout). Strangely, the dilapidated structure was embellished with a sizable and impressive assortment of antiques and collectibles—a large oak dining-room table with a carved sideboard, marble-topped dressers and chests, ornate stands for boots and umbrellas. The people whom my wife and I encountered as we were shown the premises by Joan evoked the same reaction as the building: amazement and disorientation. There was Joan—a gaunt chain smoker who was almost totally disabled by lung ailments. There was an unwed mother and her child, who lived there. There was her brother, an engineering student, who did not. They had voluntarily chosen to leave the People's Temple prior to the mass exodus to Guyana. They had a huge family which had opted for life in Jones's jungle paradise. There was the "director" or house mother of the facility—a blond, blue-eyed college dropout and former furniture rental salesperson who had befriended the brother and sister and for then-unexplained reasons had made their lives and causes her own and had followed them to the Bay Area.

Joan called the meeting to order around the large oak table in the dining room. Our hosts, and the centerpiece of attention, were Al and Jeannie Mills, former leaders of the Temple who were current leaders of anti-Jones agitation. Jeannie was a not unattractive brunette in her late thirties. She seemed a warm, motherly person. I found her enthusiasm a bit overprojected. Her husband was about fifteen years her senior and seemed like a gentle, likable person. He went on endlessly about Jim Jones "the master manipulator" and related vicious, outrageous, and sickening humiliations which Jones had visited upon his followers—particularly upon the Millses' compatriots on the "PC" (the thirty-member Planning Commission). Al horrified me with a story of a male PC member who had been ordered to have oral sex with a black female PCer who was menstruating. I was bothered by a tone of glee in Al's voice as he recounted each disgusting episode.

While we discussed the bestiality of the defectors' former God and the need for educating the public about the dangers of "destructive cultism," a man and a woman clad in pajamas and robes, whose presence no one offered to explain, wandered aimlessly around the building quietly talking to themselves. I wondered if they were "cult victims." I learned much later that they were board and care patients left over from the days in which the Millses had operated the Regent Street house as a licensed nursing home. One—a woman in her late fifties, I would estimate—held her bathrobe tightly around her and interrupted Jeannie from time to time with requests of some sort which Jeannie brushed aside with a syrupy phrase or two and a wave of her hand. The other patient, a grinning young male schizophrenic like those in the social rehabilitation programs which I directed for six years, sat at the table with us and giggled, now and then picking up a word or two from our super-serious conversation and constructing an imaginative rhyme, e.g., "Moonie—loony."

The meeting was without agenda, focus, or clear purpose, often disturbed by the psychotics and tinged with an air of unexplained hostility. Despite the chaos, I had learned much about the People's Temple, about the kind of people it attracted, and above all, about plans on the part of the Concerned Relatives for a fact-finding mission to Jonestown which was to depart in two days under the leadership of Representative Leo Ryan—my own congressman and a slight acquaintance. I had chaired a debate between Ryan and a lackluster Republican opponent in 1976 shortly after my arrival in California. The audience was human service agency personnel from the public and private sector. The convening committee of United Way agency directors had feared being tarnished by association with politics, which was considered particularly dirty in the early post-Watergate years, and having discovered that I had been active politically—as a member of the national presidential campaign staff of U.S. Senator Henry M. ("Scoop") Jackson and as state campaign manager for a candidate for the Republican Senate nomination in Oregon—had recruited this newcomer who, I must confess, evidenced a decided preference for his fellow Democrat and social activist, Ryan.

The air of unreality of our afternoon with the HFC clashed discordantly with my feeling that something had to be done and as soon as possible. For although my wife and I found this collection of misfits among the ruins to be less than totally credible, their tales of "White Nights" or mass suicide rehearsals terrified us. Monday morning found me en route to Leo Ryan's district office, which was conveniently located a few hundred yards from mine in a San Mateo office campus. I had decided that I wanted to accompany Ryan and the Concerned Relatives to Guyana. For I was afraid that Jones would orchestrate a public relations dog and pony show for the congressional delegation and that nothing would be learned. Also I did not entirely trust my congressman. I found him rather theatrical and superficial. And so I was offering my services as a trained participative observer who could help Ryan discover whether the sensational allegations were true and whether the threat of a mass suicide was real. I went to that office with copies of my professional résumé and my publications—as though I were applying for an academic position! I was afraid that I would be dismissed as a paranoid nut, as I had shortly before miscategorized Claire Bouquet. No one in a position of authority was available, so I explained my offer to two clerical employees and left. At about the same time, the Ryan–Concerned Relative party was departing for Georgetown, Guyana, by commercial jet plane from JFK Airport in New York. I returned to my work, unaware that my message had been transmitted to Ryan via his Washington, D.C., office and that I had been cleared to come along. But no confirmation had reached me.

JONESTOWN AND AFTER

November 18, 1978. Fanaticism's Pearl Harbor. A day which will just as surely live in infamy. An event which will never be fathomed. A community of more than nine hundred men, women, and children terminated itself forever. It was a Saturday afternoon and I busied myself around the house while an unattended television blared away. And then I became aware of news bulletins about a shooting at an airstrip not far from Jonestown. No details were available. I immediately phoned the Human Freedom Center in Berkeley, wondering if they had heard the same reports or if they had any further information. I reached the "director," who told me that she was aware of the reports and asked me to relinquish the line so that concerned parties could get through. I complied. Soon enough we would all know the whole grisly story. And within a month, my life as director of a mental health association would end and my career as counselor of individuals and families disturbed by cults would begin.

First came the frantic calls from the Human Freedom Center, seeking advice and assistance as survivors, earlier People's Temple defectors, relatives of the dead, and media personages from every quarter of the globe converged upon the Regent Street house. In response to a not irrational fear of reprisals against the Concerned Relatives and against those few people who had escaped the Jonestown holocaust, a heavily armed SWAT team was posted. It was reported to me by the director of the Human Freedom Center that Jim Cobb, one of the Concerned Relatives, was seriously ill, apparently with some tropical ailment contracted during his visit to the Jonestown encampment and his subsequent headlong flight into the swampy area adjacent to the Port Kaituma airstrip, where Ryan and the other members of his party—newsmen, Concerned Relatives, that day's complement of fresh defectors, Ryan's aide (Jacqueline Speier), et al.—had been ambushed. Berkeley physicians, including two I phoned myself, refused to treat Cobb for fear of reprisals by the phantom death squad believed by many to be on the loose.

A month of nonstop talking ensued at the HFC. It was never-ending group therapy, with the survivors, the pre-massacre defectors, and the bereaved relatives coming and going, being interviewed, photographed, tape-recorded, and filmed

again and again. Questions ranging from insightful and compassionate to insensitive and cruel were asked endlessly by
reporters from France, Norway, Sweden, England, etc., *ad nauseam*. Novelists and nonfiction writers tripped over one another making special deals with the survivors (especially the
"Basketball Team," Jones's own son Stephan and his multira-
cial adopted sons and their friends).

During the first few months after Jonestown, I was able to
counsel about one third of the survivors, and I have continued
with some of them over the intervening years. Between late
November 1978 and July 1979, I heard the horrors of the
People's Temple recounted on a daily basis as I attempted to
console escapees, defectors, and relatives of the dead. I heard
stories about Jim Jones from more sources than I can remember, including tales from associates who had spent twenty
years with him. I was privy to recordings of his sermons, firsthand recollections of Temple leaders as well as rank-and-file
followers, bootlegged tapes of his phone conversations, un-
published and perhaps never to be published details of his
activities shared with me by journalists, government officials,
and others. I devoted days to counseling suddenly direc-
tionless young adults who had spent almost their entire lives
under Jones's influence.

Somehow I managed, for the most part, to keep emotional
distance between myself and the tragedy. I listened, analyzed,
categorized, and did what I could to help. I was impressed by
Jones the brilliant manipulator who had so skillfully woven
together so many diverse strands of religious and sociopoliti-
cal thought. His claims to be God and his use of the title
"Father" were purloined from Father Divine's Peace Church.
His concept of divinity as a potential present in each person
and powerfully manifest in some such as himself borrowed
heavily from New Thought and "positive thinking." His notion that God incarnates himself in each era in a community
which re-creates the miracles of Jesus and the Apostles combined Anglo-Catholic sacramentalism and Pentecostalism. His
use of the Bible to provide proof texts as pretexts was learned
from many revivalistic tent evangelists and independent Bible

churches. The use of healings and speaking in tongues was derived from the charismatic/deliverance movement. His magic tricks, such as his gift of discernment or mind reading, were taught to him by former associates of midwestern spiritualists. He studied group persuasive techniques in National Training Laboratory experiments in which he took part in the fifties. His "apostolic socialism" came from the "communism" of the Jerusalem church of the Book of Acts and his lifelong fascination with Marxism-Leninism. His style of leadership, such as the creating of four warring factions of middle management, all of which reported to him, suggests Hitler's Third Reich as its inspiration. His use of civil rights, nuclear terror, racism, sexism, and ageism as background for his creation of a hopeful vision of the future demonstrated his ability to read the needs of the times and to manipulate them for his purposes. But his was a brilliant mind undone by sadism, drug addiction, and a total inability to tolerate resistance. He had the need to be in control of others, to be the total focus of their deeds and thoughts, to have their lives and deaths in his hands. He was a monster of depravity who delighted in debauching the innocent and making his closest associates as corrupt as he was. His hypochondria had led him to an uncontrolled use of antibiotics which had destroyed his body's immunological system. His nervous system was ravaged by dependence on powerful chemical substances. It is estimated that, had he survived the jungle apocalypse, he would have been dead within days. Just when he crossed the line between (a) his calculated use of the *threat* of mass suicide with which he blackmailed the government of Guyana and tested the dedication of his followers and (b) the decision to destroy the nearly one thousand souls who had committed themselves to his despotic rule, cannot be determined.

Although the details of Jones's reign in his jungle utopia were revolting and unprecedented for the press, the government, and social service professionals, there was something about Jones which was disconcertingly familiar to me. Two decades of study of "fringe religious phenomena" had led me to many People's Temples and numerous Jim Joneses—storefront missions with their archbishops, independent churches with their apostles, sects and cults with their gods, gurus, and messiahs. And I had met many abject subjects ready and willing to do the will of their self-proclaimed prophets and prophetesses. Fortunately, the unique combination of factors which permitted a Jonestown has not repeated itself on such a scale. But it could.

And then one rainy evening in March 1979, my composure fell apart. I was driving on the San Mateo Bridge, a ten-mile-long span, on my way home. The previous night I had been present when survivors and defectors had gathered with an NBC crew to examine videotapes which had been shot during the Ryan mission to Jonestown. As the tapes were shown repeatedly at freeze-frame speed, the survivors and defectors named all the persons who appeared on the screen. At the time, many of the victims, particularly the children, were unidentified. Driving across the Bay, I began thinking again about the dead in Jonestown. I reflected, somewhat heartlessly, that they all would have died anyway, sooner or later, and that had it not been for their slavish devotion, their lives would probably have meant nothing. The dream of Jonestown had given them life and had taken it from them.

Suddenly my mind shifted to the dead children, the three hundred incipient human stories which had been snuffed out. I had never shed a tear for the fathers and the mothers, the grandparents, the husbands and the wives, the crafty and the outfoxed—Jonestown's big people. Jones twisted their arms and mangled their minds while drawing his strength from their abject weakness. I had never cried for them. But when I thought of the deaths of three hundred little ones—"Dad's nursery," the Temple's tomorrow that was never to be—when I thought of them, I ached as though someone had just announced my death.

As I drove on, my hands tightened on the steering wheel, and I began to scream, "Sometime, somewhere, someone must accept responsibility! If the God I worship and love and serve—if this God deceives and defrauds, then I must own up and say that it is my own fault—that I gave him the power to

destroy and I must accept the blame." "It is all so simple," I
thought. "Accept responsibility for your own life, and let God
be God." And for five years, these words have governed my
work and served as my advice to my clients.

FREEDOM COUNSELING CENTER—

AN INNOVATIVE APPROACH

It was not only the public fascination with the macabre demise
of the People's Temple but other events, both of a personal
and private nature, which led me to found Freedom Counseling Center. I had just completed seven years as a political
campaign consultant and as a mental health administrator,
seven years away from my true area of interest—religious experience. And I wanted to return. Second, there was my concern about a virtual war on nontraditional, authoritarian, innovative, and/or communal religions which was declared the day
after Jonestown. Suddenly anything strange became suspect.
Every cult, sect, and occult group became a potential Jonestown. Panic overcame reason. Deprogrammings multiplied.
Cults resisted with increasing vigor. The deprogrammers and
other anticultists became more violent. The atrocity stories of
ex-members of several groups became commonplace. And the
media repeated them without examining their authenticity or
questioning the motives of their bearers just as it accepted the
stock tales of the Jonestown–People's Temple storytellers
without exploring the self-serving nature of much that was
disclosed. Former Moonies alone would account for at least a
dozen potboilers. Jonestown became the most powerful negative metaphor in twentieth-century religious history. Its power
would not be lost on non-deprogrammed cult members, many
of whom on their own reevaluated their commitments to
movements headed by charismatic leaders who claimed the
same immunity from rational examination and the same
unquestioning obedience as Jones did. Defections were more
common than the Anticult Network has ever realized. (For an

explanation of the Anticult Network [ACN], see chapters 8, 9, and 10.)

I am by nature, training, and experience disdainful of fanaticism—whether that fanaticism is the unreasoning bombast of self-appointed messiahs or the call for the suspension of civil liberties demanded by the enemies of "destructive cultism." I also am deeply touched by the pain and bewilderment which characterizes the loss of faith. And as I believed that my being available as a sympathetic listener and as a reminder of forgotten options had been of value to the Jonestown survivors, so I hoped I could prove a guide to other ex-cultists as they sought to redirect their lives. It was my desire to help families which had been sundered by religious differences, to provide them with insights rather than scare stories, to help them develop appropriate strategies for reconciliation. I wanted to counsel cult members, to stimulate them to think outside the narrow confines of ideological clichés, easy answers for everything, proof texts cited by chapter and verse—just as Miss T. and Charley had urged me to be both true to my faith while being my authentic self. And I wanted to do this without resorting to violence, compulsion, or deception. And, finally, I wanted to help former believers, no matter how they had lost faith, to see that there is life after cult, that it is possible to separate the wheat of basic living truths from the chaff of self-delusion and go on with one's own life. At the beginning of 1979, this was only a wish list supported by a number of unexamined presuppositions. It was the articles of faith of a yet untried experiment.

I rented an office in Burlingame, near San Francisco International Airport. I ordered the mandatory business cards. I prepared a brief, inexpensive brochure which described "an Innovative Counseling Service to assist individuals to accept responsibility for their own lives." I mailed the brochures to every minister and mental health professional in my county. I described the new service when I was interviewed on local talk shows. I was invited to speak to my own Rotary Club and to a few other groups and college classes. Next I placed a small classified ad in the "announcement" section of the two San Francisco dailies, the *Chronicle* and the *Examiner:*

> HELP for individuals and families disturbed
> by cults. Weekdays 9 to 5. 697-6737.

I told myself that I was conducting an experiment to determine the need for specialized services including counseling, supportive listening, information, and referral for individuals and families disturbed by authoritarian religious groups. I felt that I was qualified to render such services on the basis of my several books, lecturing, and consultant work that I had done in the past on small innovative religious groups such as the "Jesus people," my Princeton University doctorate in religious experience, my eight years as a teacher of contemporary religious movements at Temple University, my six years of hands-on mental health experience as the administrator of community programs in Delaware and California, my ordination as a minister in the United Church of Christ, and, last but not least, my informal counseling during the previous fifteen years of more than three hundred individuals in transition both from "normal" society to religious groups and from religious groups to "normal" life.

I began answering the phone on January 8, 1979. It has rung constantly ever since.

TED PATRICK AND THE CHILDREN OF GOD

One final beginning is relevant to what follows in these pages. It does not directly involve the author as much as it does a former truck driver and minor California state employee named Theodore Roosevelt Patrick. In the early 1970s, when the covers of *Time* and *Newsweek* were plastered with pop renditions of "Jesus Christ Superstar" and the media were atwitter with something called "the Jesus revolution," "Jesus people," and "Jesus freaks," Ted Patrick was enjoying a quiet day at the beach with his family. His teenage son wandered off and re-

turned in a disoriented state as a result of an encounter with an
ultrafundamentalist band of proselytizers from a group known
as the Children of God. (At about the same time and not far
away, I was spending the day with COGers at their "colony" at
a warehouse in the skid row section of Los Angeles.) The
younger Patrick's strange behavior—his "zombielike" gait and
his "thousand yard" stare—suggested to Ted that his son had
been drugged or hynotized.

After receiving numerous complaints about the Children of
God at the governor's office in San Diego, where Patrick was
employed, Patrick decided to investigate for himself. (I had
also heard numerous complaints of their overzealous and un-
ethical actions throughout the Jesus people communities of
California as I researched my book *The Jesus Trip: Advent of the
Jesus Freaks.* So I also decided to investigate for myself.)
Dressed in old clothes, which he believed made him look like a
derelict but which probably were indistinguishable from the
"street Christian" or "urban guerrilla" fashion then in vogue,
the middle-aged, short, black, semi-articulate (he has a pronounced speech impediment and a cliché-ridden, limited vo-
cabulary) Patrick allowed himself to be picked up by the
young, white, highly verbal COGers and indoctrinated. Their
endless exhortations and recitations of Bible passages had the
same effect on him as he had noted earlier upon his son. He
became mesmerized and felt that he was losing his mind. As he
tells the story, it was only by the most heroic effort that he was
able to undo COG's spell and escape before becoming a
"mindless robot."

My own experience at a COG colony was radically different.
When the COGers asked me questions ("Are you saved?"
"Have you received the Spirit?" etc.), I answered them directly. When they preached at me, I stood my ground and
indicated my areas of agreement and disagreement. When
several people surrounded me and tried to overwhelm me with
their biblical recitals, I simply focused upon a single member
of the group and shut out the rest. I found them charming,
naïve, and simpleminded—but scarcely capable of robbing me

of the exercise of my free will. It was boredom which compelled me to leave—not fear for my sanity.

The roots of my disagreement with Ted Patrick and with the technique of forcible deconversion which he introduced and which has come to be known as "deprogramming" can be traced, in part, to our divergent reactions to a similar experience. But there is much more than this pair of incidents which sets us apart. To say this is truly to begin.

2

What Is a Cult?

A month after Jonestown, I founded a counseling service for "individuals and families disturbed by cults." Five years later, the service, Freedom Counseling Center, continues as virtually America's only professional agency wholly dedicated to assisting individuals and families whose lives have been disturbed by cults, sects, and other authoritarian groups. During the past five years, we have worked with nearly two thousand families from every part of the world, who have come to seek our help as a result of something or other in their lives which they designated "cult." In addition, I have personally been involved in cases in more than half the states in this country and in Canada, England, South Africa, and Japan.

CHARACTERISTICS OF CULTS

What exactly is a cult? The term "cult" does not have a precise scientific meaning. Webster's Dictionary defines "cult" as follows: "1. A system of religious worship or ritual. 2. Devoted attachment to or extravagant admiration for, a person, a principle, etc., especially when regarded as a fad; as, the *cult* of nudism. 3. A group of followers; sect." It is the problem of *excessive* or *fanatic* devotion which concerns Freedom Counseling Center. When we speak of cults, we are referring to certain kinds of authoritarian religious movements that tend to disrupt the lives of involved followers and, thus, become a subject of concern to family members or friends of these followers. The groups with which we deal as counselors share common characteristics:

A cult is a *nontraditional* religious group based upon the teachings of an *authoritarian* leader. A single individual is the sole source of what the group believes and of the rules that govern daily behavior. The leader may claim that he is interpreting or rediscovering some ancient tradition, but he is *innovative* and *idiosyncratic.* No matter how much his system of doctrine may be derived from other sources, it is perceived by its adherents as *original* and *unique.*

A cult is a *highly structured, strictly disciplined* group that demands the total time, dedication, and resources of its members. Further, a cult has the means to enforce its demands. Usually, embarrassing wayward members before their peers or making them feel guilty about their lack of dedication is sufficient. In extreme cases, cults engage in beatings, forced confinement, threats of bodily harm, and, in rare instances, murder.

A cult sees itself as the *only possessor of truth* and regards those outside the cult as unsaved, unenlightened, unspiritual, and hostile to the truth. Many cults are *apocalyptic.* They see these as the last days and themselves as the elite which will overcome unbelievers and rule the world. They anticipate a time of persecution and warfare before they attain their goals. Some millenarian groups take their fantasies of impending doom quite seriously and are moving to the wilderness, stockpiling foodstuffs, and practicing military maneuvers with arsenals of assault weapons.

Primary cult activities are *new-member recruitment* and *fund raising.* Cults may claim all manner of social-betterment and educational activities, but in most cases these turn out to be forms of evangelism or acquiring money for the group itself.

Cult initiation techniques are frequently based upon *deception* and *psychological manipulation.* In many cases, potential recruits are misled about the true identity of the group and about the true purpose of its activities. They are brought into totally controlled, secluded environments where they are subjected to the bombardment of strange new ideas, the constant pressure of peer approval or rejection, physical exhaustion, unusual or poor diet, and the induction of phobias concerning their lives, work, friends, and family.

Most cults employ systematic forms of *consciousness-altering practices* (chanting, speaking in tongues, listening to hours of boring tape recordings, recitation of memorized material, etc.) that make individuals suggestible to group dictates and group control rather than to self-determination.

Money is often obtained under *false pretenses*. Cult fund raisers frequently solicit for services which their respective groups allegedly provide but which, in fact, do not exist (orphanages, drug abuse programs, scholarships for students, hospitals, hunger relief), and they have been known to use the names of established, accepted groups such as UNICEF, campus ministries, the Bicentennial Commission, etc.

Members of cults are encouraged to *cut off communications* with family members and friends.

Cultists allow the group leader to make *important decisions* concerning career and marriage for them.

In many instances, cult members give their possessions and earnings to the group and, in turn, become *totally dependent* on the group.

There is, to be sure, a great variety in theology, ethics, organization, living arrangements, diet, costume, etc., from group to group. Some are sects—that is, they have splintered off from established groups. Others are as original as anything human can be. But, in general, the above characteristics describe the sort of phenomena with which we deal at Freedom Counseling Center. Unlike some commentators, I feel that the term "cult" is useful—as long as its meaning is stipulated. It is no less precise than "religion" or "love" or "America." For several months in 1979, I avoided the word entirely, out of respect for my scholarly associates (who prefer "sect" and "nontraditional religion") and for fear that I would bias the public against specific groups while Jonestown was still fresh in their collective memory. I have been told that my books *The Cults Are Coming!* and *Cults* add to popular prejudice by their very titles. Yet I cannot imagine a publisher approving a title like *The Innovative, Authoritarian, Totalistic, Totalitarian, Elitist, Nontraditional Religious Groups with a Wide Variety of Theologies, Ethics, and Lifestyles Are Coming!* Generalizations are always dangerous but without them very little can be said.

THE SIMPLE EXCHANGE

Cults are based on a simple exchange. The individual surrenders all that he has, is, and will be. In return, the leader gives him easy answers for complex personal and social problems. Who is attracted to this simple swap? The weak? The mentally ill? There is a common misconception that cults attract loners, weirdos, and freaks. But that is not true. The people whom I meet who are attracted to cults are more "normal" than they are "abnormal." The average cult recruit, on the basis of my experience, is twenty-three years of age, has three and a half to five years of college training, and is having a difficult time in assuming adult responsibilities, usually because he has lost his enthusiasm for the career he had earlier chosen or has recently broken up with a "live-in" lover/companion. A typical cult recruit is idealistic—has evidenced for some time prior to his cult experience a yearning for a better world and a willingness to invest time and energy in altruistic undertakings. The cult-inclined individual is somewhat naïve, gullible, and unstable. We note among our subjects an incidence of previous mental illness which is double that of the population as a whole. But we do not know if this is because of the age group (eighteen to thirty-three) with which we deal or because cults attract a more sensitive, alienated, and psychologically fragile clientele. The majority of our subjects have been white, male, from suburban families, and the second of three children. Young men seem extremely confused as to what is expected of them in the world of liberated women. Cults provide clear role models and unambiguous images of sexual differentiation. The cult-prone-ness of middle children probably stems from commonly ob-served mid-sibling characteristics: other-directedness, a desire to please others and fit in, an adeptness at compromise, and an inability to say no.

HOW MANY CULTS? HOW MUCH MONEY?

No one knows how many cults there are or how many members they have. The Anticult Network, a coalition of parents' groups, deprogrammers, evangelical cult watchers, and allied mental health professionals (which is described at length in chapter eight), estimates that in the United States there are more than three thousand cults with between three million and twenty million adult members. How these figures were arrived at is open to conjecture. Much depends upon what one regards as a cult as well as how membership is defined. Also there are many distortions in the data provided by groups themselves. When a group wants to appear vital and growing, it exaggerates its membership statistics. When a group desires to be seen as a tiny, harmless minority, it offers reduced esti-mates. Thus, spokesmen for one cult told me on one occasion that their group had a national membership of twenty-five thousand, but a few months later that their membership was four thousand.

Cults with which we have dealt at Freedom Counseling Center range in size from "no name" sects with three to eight members to major groups with membership in the scores of thousands. We have counseled members of more than one hundred different groups with a combined membership of about two hundred thousand. The larger, more organized groups amass enormous amounts of money, which, in turn, gives them considerable power. In most of the cults with which I am familiar, the average convert nets at least a hundred dollars a day for the group through begging on the streets, door-to-door sales of literature, flowers, candy, jewelry, pottery, seafood, etc., or by working in cult-owned business ventures. The typical recruit works more than three hundred days a year, often twelve to fourteen hours a day. Hence, a single recruit is worth about thirty thousand dollars a year (300 days × $100 a day) to the group. One thousand recruits can produce more than thirty million dollars a year.

With this money, cults are able to purchase real estate, businesses, automobiles, airplanes, farms, and raw materials. They are in a position to disrupt the free-enterprise marketplace by overbidding in order to deny supplies to their competition and by underbidding when they offer services. What can Del Monte do when the fishing catch is bought at top dollar by a cult-owned packing firm? How can a janitorial service or a painting contractor compete with a group which has no labor costs? Further, limitless cash buys influence in the political and judicial spheres. Candidates who are amenable to the policies of a given group are favored with campaign contributions as well as the services of dedicated, round-the-clock volunteers. Conversely, public officials who resist such groups by calling for investigations of their activities or sponsoring restrictive legislation become the victims of well-financed, cult-organized smear campaigns. Some cults hire infiltrators to spy on their critics, including counselors, writers, anticult groups, and government agencies. Parents and anticult professionals are lured into conspiracies with deprogrammers so that the cult may press onerous and costly criminal and civil proceedings. Free speech, the publication of books and magazine articles, and open discussion are chilled by nuisance suits for libel and defamation.

The first criticism made of an emerging religious sect in America has to do with its finances. Our society, which so idolizes monetary success in other spheres, applies a strange standard to spiritual movements. Poverty and purity are somehow regarded as identical. At least critics of religion are fair. They are as likely to fault the Roman Catholic Church for its conspicuous collection of art treasures and real estate as they are to count the number of Mercedes-Benzes and beachside condominiums owned by a self-proclaimed messiah. The adherents of cults are models of sacrificial asceticism. Not only do they give up everything to follow their faith—give it up to the group—but their lives are given in large measure to raising funds for the cult. They are clearly not in it for the money.

And neither are most of the cult and sect leaders with whom I am familiar. They are after something more important than money—power. And in our society, money is power's most tangible symbol. Many of today's founder-prophets, gurus, and gods flaunt spectacular wealth. They live like maharajahs, movie stars, and Greek shipping magnates. They live in luxury while the faithful sacrifice comfort, security, proper diet, and adequate medical attention.

Such disparity is justified by several myths which are espoused in group after group. First, the leader is "entitled" to special honors because of who and what he is. Special status in the divine order of things deserves exceptional honors in the earthly sphere. The leader asks nothing for himself. The followers vie with one another to give freely whatever they can to him. They are motivated by a deep sense of gratitude and they try to win favor in the eyes of their leader as well as their peers. Second, material goods are viewed as small rewards for the sufferings which the leader has allegedly endured in the past and the superhuman efforts which he expends in his current office as mediator between God and man. Third, material things are of no importance; the accumulation of them by the leader is for the sake of his ministry to unbelievers—to impress them with the extent to which the leader enjoys the favor of God. "If Jesus were alive today," a Unification Church fund raiser asked me, "wouldn't you expect him to wear fine clothes and be driven around in a Rolls-Royce? How else could he make a good impression on the United Nations delegates and world leaders?" Fourth, it is all a joke. The master surrounds himself with materialistic geegaws so that he can show the world how unimportant they really are. Fifth, the leader's acquisition of the things of this world is really his way of winning back for God what Satan has stolen from him.

Finally, the amassing of vast wealth is justified on the grounds that the properties, vehicles, publishing houses, and businesses of the group belong not to the leader but to the movement and, hence, to each of its individual members. What glorifies the leader brings honor to them. The whole world belongs to God, Christ, or Krishna, they reason. Why should the Landlord of Creation allow his chosen servant to wallow in squalor.

THE WORSHIP OF THE FOUNDER

Without question, the founder-prophet is worshipped. The nonbeliever may find the leader unattractive, even unimpressive, and he may consider the reverence of a human being an act of idolatry. But unconditional devotion to the leader resolves intense conflicts for the devotee. I have noted again and again the tendency of my clients/subjects to engage in a devastating personal psychodrama. First, as members of the group, they experience a profound sense of loss, such as the death of a loved one or the end of a friendship or the disorientation of being transferred from a familiar post to an unknown location. They become disoriented and despondent—until two contrasting images crystallize in their consciousnesses. On the one side is their own shameful unworthiness. On the other is an idealized and exaggerated picture of the leader as wise, spiritually perfected, caring, and loving. The devotee lets go of his self-deprecation and loses himself in rapture. Thoughts of the perfect master fill the emptiness of his life, crowding out his sadness and loneliness. He feels at one with the leader. His bliss overflows in heightened awareness of the sensory data which surround him. Suddenly the grass is greener; the sky bluer; each breath sweeter than ever before. Every mundane experience is transformed into an encounter with the divine. Some devotees report psychedelic states—visual and auditory hallucinations. The pain of dislocation is gone. And the leader is responsible—or so the worshipful convert believes.

What is going on in the mind of the person who worships a cult leader? He has been exposed to some personal trauma

that has thrown him out of balance emotionally. He has subli-
mated his instinctual responses. He has chosen to deal with a
projected image, the founder-prophet, rather than with the
real cause of the upheaval. The redirection of his feelings has
produced a sense of intense relief, release, and purification, in
consequence of which he has found his senses stimulated and
the everyday world transfigured. Similar experiences are reported to me by individuals who fall in love, who are born
again, who turn on through the use of psychedelic drugs, who
achieve a breakthrough or a peak experience in a therapy
group, who get "it" at the est Training, who realign their
chakras through Kundalini Yoga, or who become "clear"
through Scientology auditing.

The pattern of response to the object of these forms of
experience is identical. The goal of each form of worship is
identity with or possession by the elusive other (God, the
Beloved, the Leader, enlightenment, etc.). Within the context
of the authoritarian religious group, the Leader is experienced
by the devotee as both *numinous* and *charismatic.* According to
Rudolf Otto's classic description, the holy, or numinous, is
"wholly other." It is "quite beyond the sphere of the usual, the
intelligible, and the familiar." It is a "living force," an almost
electric energy that fills the individual by whom it is felt with
both fascination and dread. A tension is created that can never
be resolved. The individual is attracted to a communion that
transforms his life. At the same time, he is overpowered with a
sense of obligation and unworthiness.[1]

The intensity of the experience and the totality of the demands which are felt are inseparable. As Joachim Wach observes, religious experience is a "total response of the total
being to what is apprehended as ultimate reality . . . the
most intense experience of which man is capable."[2] In the
Judeo-Christian heritage, such experiences pertain to God
alone. But, I would argue, religious experience differs in degree rather than in kind from experiences of other powerful
affective states. The first meeting of the lover and the beloved
is also filled with awe—terror mingled with fascination. The
leader of a mass movement and the very concepts and slogans

upon which the movement is based strike the follower with a sense of reverence—a feeling of personal unworthiness combined with a deep sense of obligation. There is a curious duality about a sacred cause. On the one hand, there is a fascination which lures us to oneness, while, at the same time, there is a discomfort which distances us from the object of our veneration characterize mankind's most precious pursuits.

CHARISMA

When a leader of a cult or sect strikes us with fascination and dread, we speak of that person as "charismatic." Despite the abuse of the word "charisma" in recent years—it is even the name of a perfume—it is an extremely valuable concept for the understanding of religious experience and its surrogates. According to Max Weber, charisma is

> a certain quality of an individual personality by virtue of which he is set apart from ordinary men and treated as endowed with supernatural, superhuman, or at least specifically exceptional powers or qualities. These are such as are not accessible to the ordinary person, but are regarded as of divine origin, or as exemplary. And on the basis of them the individual concerned is treated as a leader.[3]

Clearly, charisma is the possession by an individual of "numinousity" or "wholly otherness." By virtue of charisma, the individual becomes an object of religious experience, romantic love, or the center of a new social reality. Does the object of devotion really possess "exceptional powers or qualities"? Or does charisma exist chiefly in the eye of the beholder? (Ask forty thousand wildly cheering, gyrating fans at a rock concert.) Charisma is the meeting of objective characteristics and subjective needs. The more intensely dissatisfied the individual is, the more he will project upon the mysterious other (be it loved one, star, candidate, deity, or movement) those qualities he finds most lacking in himself.

Is it necessary for there to be "something there," some basis for the projection? I used to think so. Today I am not so sure. Believers rely upon a peculiar alchemy that not only turns lead into gold—it turns used Kleenex into gold. Loyalty born of desperation can overlook inconsistencies, malevolence, cowardice, theft, sexual perversion, greed, and insanity. Much faith, of course, is blind faith that expects of its object what its object can never provide. For the more ignorant we are of our beloved, our leader, or our God at the time we make the brave and dangerous leap of self-commitment, the more we are able to suppress doubt and receive self-fulfillment in return for self-surrender. The blanker the screen, the more that can be projected upon it.

In the realm of everyday life, rumors can be dispelled by facts. Reputations can be destroyed by adverse publicity. Heroes can be dethroned by newer heroes. Stars can be robbed of their allure. But the worship of the charismatic leader is highly resistant to the usual sources of disenchantment. It makes no difference what the facts are. The need to believe is so great for the cultist that he will ignore all that tends to discredit the founder-prophet. Media attention to Sun Myung Moon, for instance, has been overwhelmingly hostile. He is depicted as a tool of the South Korean government, a present-day Hitler, a discredited heretic who was excommunicated from the church of his youth, a lecher, a rip-off artist who has reaped millions from his underfed and overworked disciples. Such attacks are well known among the Moonies. In 1978, I predicted that if "Moon were tomorrow convicted of stock manipulation or Mann Act violations and sentenced to prison, the hard core of his followers would simply dismiss the reality of the situation as Satan's attack upon God's chosen messenger."[4] Moon has since been convicted of tax fraud for failing to report as personal income the dividends which he received on stocks. He maintains that he only accepted the funds as trustee for the Unification Church. His appeal has been rejected and, barring higher court reversal, he could end up in a federal penitentiary.

The response of his church has been predictable. Moon is seen as a martyr who is being persecuted by the government because he heads an unpopular religion, is Korean and Oriental. There has been no mass exodus from the Unification Church since his conviction. However, I would not infer that the movement has not suffered a loss of credibility in the eyes of its supporters, friends, and potential converts. Using conviction for tax fraud as proof of one's divine calling has its limitations. Civil punishment for relatively minor offenses has a way of reducing the charismatic leader to the level of ordinary human beings and piercing the veil of alleged superhuman character. Arresting a religious leader for violations of dog license requirements is more harmful to his image than accusing him of murder.

The true believer is desperate for structure, order, and authority. Apart from the identity and support of the group, the life of the individual is lonely and trivial. Projecting charisma even where it has little foundation is a way of sharing reality with that which is worshipped. If I make the object of my devotion worthy of my devotion, I become more significant and real than if I believed in nothing or merely accepted human beings at face value. The true believer is one who cannot *not* believe. He believes in belief itself.

Cults act as though they are above the law. They believe that they are accountable only to a "higher authority." Most cults believe that their leader is God, the messiah, or God's only authorized spokesman. Each group believes that it alone has the truth, that it is destined to rule the world, and that it is furthering the divine plan by deceiving, stealing, defrauding, and manipulating for its purposes. The moral landscape of cult mentality has only one fixed point of reference: The ends justify the means.

THE FUNCTIONS OF CULTS

Do cults serve any useful functions? Do they have any value? If not, they would not exist. Cults arise from dissatisfaction with the way the world is and from visions of how it ought to be. They provide a sense of identity and direction to individuals who without cults lack a sense of purpose and fixed values. If one contrasts young people who are involved in a cause with those who simply live egocentric lives, there is something very attractive about their enthusiasm, discipline, and dedication. Among cult members whom I have known over long periods of time, I have witnessed personal gains in impulse control, self-respect, interpersonal communication skills, and persistence in pursuing goals. Former dopers now "turn on to God"; the promiscuous have become celibate; indolent drifters have become hardworking zealots. (I have also known non-users who became drug-and-God-obsessed addicts; sexual prudes who became "hookers for Jesus"; and dedicated graduate students who meditated their way into academic failure.) Conversion to a cult can release previously untapped reservoirs of personal talent and ability. For many individuals, conversion marks the beginning of a spiritual quest which lasts a lifetime, and which takes them to ever higher and more integrative levels of existence. Unfortunately, the usual pattern is not one of growth. All too often, the cost of being in a cult is giving up the right to be oneself. Converts become very deindividualized. Their conceptual ability shrinks. Their speech becomes cliché-ridden. Their personalities atrophy. Instead of undergoing a liberating rite of passage, they appear trapped at an immature stage of development. And whatever gains the convert makes, he makes them in an atmosphere which is essentially exploitative, destructive of individuality, antifamily, and dishonest. Finally, there is the added danger of the fanatic group: its self-justifying morality, its sense of itself as possessing a monopoly on the truth and of outsiders as its enemies, and its paranoid fantasies of the future, which constitute an ever-present potential for violence.

3

The Cult That Never Was

We are often contacted by people who yearn for us to declare a given group a "brainwashing cult" so that they may absolve themselves of the guilt which they feel in response to a loved one's involvement or their own previous involvement. Others look upon us as an "objective source" which can either confirm their suspicions or allay their anxieties about a given group.

Not every nontraditional or idiosyncratic group concerns us. There are many communal sectarian groups about which we have never heard a complaint. And there are responsible, open, cooperative sects and cults which disdain the excesses of other groups, actively encourage dialogue between recruits and the outside world, and value the constructive criticism of nonbelievers. We would certainly have to express our appreciation of groups which have been helpful and considerate. I think particularly of the Holy Order of Mans, the Free Communion Church, and the Siddhi Yoga Society. In working with these three groups, I have found a genuine concern for the welfare of their members as well as a proper sense of good public relations. Unfortunately such groups appear the exceptions rather than the rule.

Freedom Counseling Center is based on a working notion of what is a cult. Equally important is having a notion of what is *not* a cult. We receive several phone calls a month from anxious parents, ministers, journalists, law enforcement officials, and others asking us if a given group is a "cult." We reply that FCC is not the Better Business Bureau of American religion. We describe for our callers the characteristics of disruptive groups, we share with them the data which we have acquired from our clients as well as from our other research, and we urge the inquirers to judge for themselves.

Accusations of cultism and brainwashing are often used to justify parental intervention in family matters which have little or nothing to do with religious issues. I have frequently refused to help clients who insisted that harmless, innocuous groups had brainwashed their children or who wanted me to help them obtain custody of minor children on the grounds that the involvement of one or both of the parents in a commune or religious sect was sufficient grounds for deeming the sect members unfit parents.

THE SURREY COMMUNITY

An FCC case in which such issues were spotlighted concerned a small religiously based community in British Columbia and the deprogramming efforts of the parents of one of the communards. The following chapter is based upon a report which I prepared for a child custody case in British Columbia. The report, in turn, has its roots in investigations which I conducted between early April and early June 1980. The report concerns a communal group or "community" consisting of six married couples and one single adult as well as four minor children. The group resides in Surrey, a suburb of Vancouver, British Columbia, Canada. The primary purposes of my investigation were to determine whether or not the community was a "cult" and whether or not accusations of child abuse within the group were true.

PERSONAL EXPERIENCES WITH THE "COMMUNITY"— APRIL AND MAY 1980

My personal involvement with the community in Surrey began a week before Easter of this year. On Tuesday, March 25, I was phoned by John Brown from Sydney, Australia. Brown expressed alarm about the involvement of his son Louis in a communal group located in Vancouver, British Columbia. Major Brown believed the group to be a cult and feared his son's mental health had been damaged by his involvement with the group. He described the group as part of the "Bubba Free John cult." He was convinced that the group was attempting to obtain the Brown family estate. I was informed that Louis and his wife, Marjorie, were expected at the Browns' home on or about April 2.

Major Brown asked me to come to Australia and to attempt to help the family resolve their disputes over the group. I reluctantly agreed. I knew very little about the Free Communion Church, Vision Mound, or the Dawn Horse Society, as the northern California communal group which follows Franklin Jones aka Bubba Free John or Da Free John is known. I was speaking at a conference in Berkeley the next day and met Randal Blake who had started a counseling service for ex-cultists. Randal told me that he had a number of clients who had defected from Vision Mound. I believed that he could be useful and invited him to join me on my trip to Australia. Before our departure, he arranged a meeting with about ten former members of Vision Mound. At the meeting I heard numerous allegations of corruption within the group, including sexual exploitation of several female members by the Guru. The picture which emerged was of a very unsavory communal situation, one characterized by capricious manipulation and avaricious exploitation of the membership.

A number of atrocity stories of the type which I hear from former members of virtually any cult organization were told. I had the feeling that I was back at a meeting of the Concerned Relatives who had attempted to call public attention to the situation in Guyana prior to Leo Ryan's ill-fated fact-finding mission. Randal also secured for me literature written by Bubba Free John and tape recordings of the Guru's lectures. The material literally put me to sleep whenever I attempted to wade through it.

INTERLUDE IN AUSTRALIA

Randal and I flew to Sydney, arriving at the Browns' home two days before our subjects. The Browns lived in a historic dwelling which was built in the early eighteenth century and is more of a public monument than a home. It had been used as the set of a motion picture on at least one occasion.

While we waited for Louis and Marjorie, we were taken for pleasant tours of the Browns' farm and the homes of their friends. One of them, a retired army major, was delighted to meet me, recognizing me as the head of a secret organization of mysterious "mission impossible" agents. With a wink, he whispered that he knew that "Streiker" was only my *nom de guerre* and that it was derived from the name of my secret organization, "Strike Force." I am sure that my denials only confirmed my identity.

When Louis and Marjorie finally arrived they seemed relieved that Randal and I were present, since they really wanted someone to mediate between Louis's parents and themselves.

Our meetings with Louis and Marjorie went from awkward to mildly tense to friendly. On the basis of three days of conversations with Louis and Marjorie Brown, Randal and I reported to the Browns that their son and daughter-in-law were *not* involved in a cult organization; that the Surrey community was a commune rather than a cult; that Louis did not seem to have been harmed by his involvement in the group; that his pursuits of a somewhat untraditional lifestyle in a commune should be regarded as a stage in his development. In addition, we were able to negotiate an understanding between the John Browns and the Louis Browns concerning the family estate and possessions. The mother and son were content with our settlement, but the father was not. He kept insisting that Louis should return to his station and duties as an apprentice beef farmer. Randal and I returned to San Francisco, and I awaited further developments, which were not long in coming.

In my conversations with the John Browns prior to the arrival of Louis and Marjorie, I learned that they had been contacted by telephone and through a personal visit by Mary Williams, the mother of Belinda Netski. Belinda, or Bella, her husband, Thomas, and their two-year-old son, Noble, were also involved in the Surrey community during the events described in this report and are still so engaged at the present time. The Browns described Mrs. Williams's behavior as highly erratic. At times she seemed quite coherent; at other times, utterly hysterical. Mrs. Williams was convinced that the group was a cult, that it was directed by the Bubba Free John organization in Clearlake Highlands, California, and that her daughter had suffered great physical and emotional humiliation at the hands of her husband and other members of the "cult." According to the Browns, Mrs. Williams believed that the group was engaged in systematic brainwashing activities, intense recruitment of new members, and obtaining funds for Bubba Free John. She stated that it was her intention to have her daughter and son-in-law abducted and "deprogrammed." It was related to me by the senior Browns that a deprogramming attempt had been aborted in early 1980 and that another attempt was about to take place coincident with the visit of their son and daughter-in-law. I expressed to the senior Browns my feeling that the activities of the Williamses were inappropriate in light of the fact that the Vancouver community consisted of individuals who had long since broken away from the Free Communion Church and whose lifestyle hardly bore the characteristics of a cult.

"BLACK LIGHTNING" STRIKES

On April 11, I was phoned by Louis Brown from Australia. Louis informed me that two members of the community, Bella and Thomas Netski, had been abducted and that the group was extremely upset. Louis asked if I would assist him and the group in locating their friends and in obtaining their release. During subsequent conversations via long-distance telephone with Henry Stevens and Roger Smith of the Surrey community, I was retained as a consultant on their behalf. Louis reported to me a telephone conversation between his parents and Mary Williams during which Mrs. Williams indicated that Bella and Thomas had been abducted by Ted Patrick and were being held in the area of Mount Vernon, Washington. A week after the abduction, I flew to San Diego, California, accompanied by Francis Hatch, M.S.W., director of counseling services at Freedom Counseling Center. Mr. Hatch was himself deprogrammed by Ted Patrick under coercive circumstances in October 1979 and had worked for Patrick before he was hired by Freedom Counseling Center. He was able to arrange for a dinner meeting composed of Patrick, Mrs. Patrick, himself, and myself.

NEGOTIATIONS IN SAN DIEGO

Patrick opened our conversation by telling me that I had been duped by the Browns and that the Surrey group was laughing at me. He freely admitted he had kidnapped Thomas and Bella Netski. He related that he was holding them against their will. He added that he was having a very difficult time due to constant interference from his client, Mary Williams, Bella's mother. Despite my protestations that the group was a commune rather than a cult, Patrick insisted that the Netskis were involved in the "Bubba Free John cult," that they had been brainwashed, and that they had suffered "permanent brain damage." He described them as "mindless robots, zombies." He contended that the group worshipped Bubba Free John, whose photographs appeared in every room of their dwellings, and that under cult notions of male supremacy the women in the group were badly abused, that they were "forced to live like pigs." Patrick further related that Mrs. Netski had been successfully deprogrammed, that she recognized that she had been "involved in a cult and had been held in a state of mind control and hypnosis." He maintained that Mr. Netski was a "hard nut to crack" but felt that it was only a matter of time until he could be broken and successfully "deprogrammed." "He's close to snapping right now," Patrick declared. Then he added the logically inconsistent remark that he was going to have to program Netski before he could deprogram him because the young man did not know that he was programmed. In other words, Patrick was telling him what he (Netski) believed so that Patrick could convince him that it was false!

Patrick anticipated that the Netskis would be held for a few weeks and that they would then be "rehabilitated" under less restrictive circumstances for an additional month or two. Patrick and I negotiated an agreement under which the Netskis would phone me at my home; I would be allowed to tape-record the conversation and play it for their friends in Canada. This was considered imperative by me, not only because of the anxiety of the Surrey community but because Mr. and Mrs. Netski had been separated from their two-year-old son, Noble. Patrick rambled on, telling me again that the Netskis had been "brainwashed, hypnotized, and mesmerized" by "the cult." He informed me that there were thousands of cult organizations in the United States, at least five thousand. He said that there were at least twenty million brainwashed individuals who had totally lost the exercise of their free wills. He added that he did not worry about competition because America is in need of at least one million deprogrammers and that there would be plenty of work for anyone who entered this field. He accused me of having told the Browns that he was a crook. I denied having said this. He became quite bitter about the criticism of his work by other deprogrammers and launched into a heated diatribe against another deprogrammer, who had started out as a Patrick assistant and who had become his chief competitor. He also made several ugly remarks about the San Diego prosecutor ("If guts were dynamite, he wouldn't have enough to blow his nose"), accusing him of being a pawn of the cults.

He made a number of assertions about an international conspiracy to overthrow America of which cults are simply a manifestation. He stated that several recent terrorist activities in various parts of the world (including the bombing of Harvey's Casino in Stateline, Nevada) were cult-motivated, that they were tests of the limits of mind control on the part of cult leaders. Cult recruitment, he reiterated repeatedly, was achieved through "on-the-spot hypnosis." He asked me about my techniques, and when I told him that I avoided coercion, he seemed incredulous. He wanted to know if my approach worked with Moonies, Hare Krishnas, and members of the Divine Light Mission. When I told him that I had enjoyed great success with each of these groups and others, and that at the very least I had usually been able to get members of the groups he mentioned to see me in a noncoercive setting, he pontificated that what I was claiming was simply impossible and that it had never happened.

In the course of our conversation, he or I would introduce the name of someone with whom we had had dealings in the anticult field, e.g., a psychologist or another deprogrammer. In each instance, Patrick would viciously attack the reputation of the individual mentioned. Every so often, he would reaffirm, "They're all the same. There's not a red penny's difference between any of 'em. They're all the same—Scientology, Synanon, TM, est, the Moonies, the Children of God, the New Testament Missionary Fellowship. They're all the same." Patrick made a large number of martyrdom statements: "I don't care what anyone says or what anyone does, I am going to keep right on doing what I'm doing. Let them put me in jail, let them shoot me. They have sued me so many times I have lost count, right now there are at least a hundred million dollars of lawsuits against me."

Approximately twenty minutes after my meeting with Patrick, he was arrested on kidnapping charges in San Diego, having been indicted by a grand jury for his role in the kidnapping of Roberta McElfish, a young woman who had left her husband and was living with friends. (I had nothing to do with his arrest.) The promised telephone conversation between the Netskis and me never took place. My overall impression of him? I found Ted Patrick the most programmed individual I had ever met. There was a certain charm to this gritty hustler who had created his own empire. Many who disagree with him believe that he is a man of unquestioned integrity who has involved himself in a sincere one-man crusade against the cults. For my own part, I do not agree. I felt that I was dealing with a fast-talking quick-buck artist with little understanding of the depths of human psychology or of religious experience. He is definitely antireligious. He told me that the Bible is the most brainwashing book ever written. Nobody should read the Bible. I am convinced that Patrick knows that he does not know and has no intention of becoming confused by the facts. To quote his March 1979 interview in *Playboy:* "The so-called experts on brainwashing make me glad I didn't go to college. Those people don't realize you don't have to use torture anymore. It is all done with love and kindness—and deception."

Unable to obtain the cooperation of Ted Patrick on behalf of the Surrey community, I then referred the group to another individual who I felt was more experienced than I in missing-persons matters. On May 8, 1980, I was phoned by Henry Stevens, who had been contacted by Thomas Netski and who knew exactly where the Netskis were being held (in a condominium in Vancouver, Washington—not far from Portland, Oregon). The authorities were reluctant to respond to such a wild story. I spoke with Jim Peters, the assistant district attorney of Clark County, Washington, and my corroboration of the allegation that the Netskis had been kidnapped led to immediate police action. Mr. Peters and sheriff's deputies visited the premises where the Netskis (now joined by their son) were being detained. The Netskis were freed and set at liberty to return to the community in Canada. My next and most recent involvement with the Surrey community was a result of a request from their counsel, Daniel A. Coin, who asked me to visit

the group and to prepare a professional evaluation for possible use in a child custody hearing.

AFTERMATH IN CANADA

Mary Williams had been awarded interim custody of Noble
Netski on April 28 by the Supreme Court of British Columbia
by petitioning the court on the basis of an affidavit sworn by
her daughter under extreme duress. In her petition, Mrs. Williams claimed that "it became clear to the petitioner that Bella
and Thomas no longer wished to be members of the cult
Bubba Free John." Yet Mrs. Williams then admits that Thomas
is "still somewhat confused in his thinking in relation to the
cult." In other words, he had not stated that he no longer
wished to be a member of the so-called Bubba Free John cult.
Mrs. Williams's references to the "Bubba Free John cult," said
in the petition to be in San Francisco, California, of which her
daughter, she alleges, has been a member for three years, are
equally contrafactual and inconsistent. A phone conversation
would have told the court that there is no such group as the
Bubba Free John cult in San Francisco. The group which dis-
turbs Mrs. Williams so much is the Free Communion Church,
which is located in Clearlake Highlands, California—a good
three-hour drive from San Francisco. Since a requirement for
membership is a direct personal relationship with Bubba Free
John, it is hard to see how Bella, who has resided in British
Columbia with her husband for most of the time she is alleged
to have been a member of the Bubba Free John cult, could
belong to the California group. As for Bella's affidavit, it
should be noted that she had been escorted under close guard
from her place of confinement in Vancouver, Washington, to
Portland, Oregon. While in a rest room, she had left a note
asking to be rescued from her captors. On April 27, well into
her third week of captivity and her eighth month of pregnancy,
on the basis of the deprogrammers' threats that she would

never be released if she did not cooperate, Bella signed a statement which read:

> . . . I am the mother of Noble Netski, who is almost 3 years old, and I myself am 25 years of age.
>
> That for three years I was a follower of Bubba Free John, who is a cult leader based in San Francisco, and during most of the time lived in a house with eleven other adults, including my husband, and with three children, including Noble . . . [in] Surrey, British Columbia, Canada.
>
> That I left this group in early April 1980, through the efforts of my parents and other individuals, and I am now satisfied that during the time of my involvement my mind was being controlled to the extent that I was incapable of exercising free will to a certain extent.
>
> That I have not seen Noble for 2 1/2 weeks and I am anxious to see him. Part of the teachings followed by this group involve breaking the mother-child bond.
>
> That I am fearful that if I return to Canada in order to recover my child that I may fall under the influence of this group again. . . .
>
> That I am presently 7 months pregnant.
>
> That I authorize my mother . . . to make application on my behalf to obtain custody of Noble in order to deliver him to me. . . .
>
> That I am presently staying with family and friends and they have volunteered to assist me with Noble, and to assist me while I rehabilitate.

Without ever having seen the young mother or her husband, the court granted the petition, and Mrs. Williams took custody of Noble—against the advice of Noble's physician, Patricia Blackshaw, M.D. (Noble was in the hospital, recuperating from the removal of splinters from his eye. He had fallen on a tree stump while playing.)

Toward the end of their six-week captivity, as the Netskis won the confidence of their jailers by feigning having been deprogrammed, they began to develop plans for escape. When nearby Mount St. Helen's erupted, Bella was about to steal a private plane from a local airport. (She is a licensed pilot.) But at the last moment she realized that she could scarcely fit behind the controls. She was by then eight months pregnant and quite large. On an excursion to a shopping center with a security guard, Tom slipped away to a public telephone and called the commune in Surrey. After the Netskis' release from their improvised prison in Vancouver, Washington, and their return to Surrey, they were interviewed by an investigator from the Royal Canadian Mounted Police. His report, dated May 20, 1980, includes the following observations:

> Both Thomas and Bella state they have had no involvement with BUBBA-FREE-JOHN or the FREE COMMUNION CHURCH [henceforth abbreviated BFJ and FCC, respectively] since 1977. The commune they exist in today appears to consist of a number of well educated young couples. In comparing their existence to the "norm" of our society the only significant difference is that of their COLLECTIVE economic situation. They formed a society in February, 1979, which is registered under the British Columbia Societies Act—"The Rainbow over the Landscape Foundation." This society has as a basis a number of individuals with similar ideas of a co-operative co-existence. They do not have a restricted religious structure, as one may worship whichever manner they see fit. Their day to day life finds the male populace working as contract painters and the women maintaining the households. They do not have a structured diet, rather eat whatever they please. Entertainment is encouraged. The social practices of "norm" society, i.e. consuming alcohol, dancing, etc., are up to each person, with no restrictions. The children will be attending public schools (at the moment one child is attending kindergarten).

The children have all received their immunization shots from the public health department.

The properties rented by this group are six acre plots of land. The NETSKIS live on a piece of six acre property . . . in Surrey. They pay $450.00 per month rent. They co-exist with two other married couples in a comfortable 3–4 bedroom home. The yard and outbuildings are well maintained. The house inside appears neat and also clean.

On the basis of discussions with various members of the group, the investigator observed that "this group is definitely influenced by the teachings of 'BUBBA-FREE-JOHN.' " He noted:

They claim they do not recognize him as the "DI-VINE" [but] rather agreed with his philosophy of human life. The church organization of BFJ called FCC is too structured and radical for this group, as being members at one time, they became dis-enchanted and have at present no contact with the church (since 1976). It appears this collection of young people broke away from the FCC with the dream of setting up their own religious themed soci-ety. It would appear their dreams have been some-what altered by the practical problems of everyday existence. At this particular time the society appears to be an economic co-operative with social and reli-gious ties threatening to disrupt the foundation.

He went on to note that group members have their own indi-vidual bank accounts, that they do not donate their personal assets to the foundation, and that Marjorie Brown's father is supportive of his daughter and her husband and has not with-held her funds from her. He offers a brief summary of his findings:

. . . they are influenced directly by the teachings of BFJ. They do not recognize BFJ as "GOD." They are not members of the FCC. The offspring are not con-

sidered the children of BFJ. Bella Netski explains that
her son "NOBLE" is the son of Thomas Netski and is
her child and neither BFJ nor her mother will take
him away. The home life appears quite "normal"
other than the matter of three couples existing under
one roof. Their attitude appears very forthright.

Finally, the investigator added a disclaimer (undoubtedly for
his own protection): "It should be noted that the information
supplied mostly results from discussions and impressions with
various members of this society. As investigators we are confident of our analysis, but must consider the possibilities and
potential of this group conspiring to make an example of 'Ted
Patrick,' therefore developing a test case in American law as to
the 'DEPROGRAMMING' method of Ted PATRICK. Also
there is a direct dislike for Mrs. Mary Williams by all members
of this foundation." In sum, the investigator gave the Surrey
community a clean bill of health, speculated that their religious ideas might somehow interfere with their commercial
enterprises, and offered a possible conspiracy theory that the
group was somehow trying to ambush Ted Patrick. Why a
small Canadian commune whose only contact with Patrick was
unsought and undesired would want to establish case law in
the United States is not further elaborated. By the way, I later
met the investigating team and can state unequivocally that
they did not seem brainwashed to me, but they certainly were
disturbed by all those photographs of BFJ and Mickey Mouse!

A VISIT TO SURREY

A week after the above report was prepared, I flew to Vancouver (Tuesday, May 27) and observed the group until Saturday
May 31. Mr. Hatch joined me on Wednesday, May 28, and was
with the group until Sunday, June 1. I was particularly interested in what he would have to say because he is a social
worker who is deeply concerned about the well-being of children and he was himself deprogrammed by Ted Patrick and

assisted him in snatches prior to our association. Even though he has distanced himself from Patrick's illegal methods, he remains a fan. With the exception of a few brief periods, I was with one or more members of the group during my entire visit. I conducted formal in-depth interviews with Henry Stevens ("Ski"), Cathy Stevens ("Bumpkin"), John Howard ("John-O"), Lolita Howard ("Chiquita"), Thomas Netski ("Stinko"), and Belinda Netski ("Bella") and had informal conversations with each member of the group ranging from a few moments to one or more hours in length. I observed the community's day-to-day existence, played with their children, ate at their tables, etc. In fact, I would say that I know this community as well as groups concerning which I have written in my published writings, such as my accounts of various "Jesus freak" communes in *The Jesus Trip* (Nashville: Abingdon, 1971).

IS THIS A CULT?

The first question with which we must deal is the obvious one: Is the Surrey community a cult? I can state unequivocally that it is not. I arrive at this conclusion by attempting to determine if a number of "cult" characteristics manifest themselves in this group. The term "cult" is pejorative. It does not have a precise scientific meaning. In my work I deal with families and individuals whose lives have been disrupted by involvement with certain kinds of religious movements. These movements share common characteristics. An explanatory list of such characteristics is presented in Chapter 2.

Using these criteria, let us ask whether or not the Surrey community is a cult. The Surrey community certainly reveres Bubba Free John, as is evidenced by the presence of photographs of Bubba in every room of the group's two rented houses in Surrey. (They also display numerous depictions of Mickey Mouse.) In addition, virtually every member of the community has at one time or another been involved either with the northern California Free Communion Church (also known as Vision Mound and the Dawn Horse Society) or with the now abandoned "seed" communities established by the Free Communion Church in Vancouver, British Columbia, or London, England. At the very least, each member of the group has been influenced by the writings of Bubba Free John, particularly his three early books, *The Knee of Listening, The Method of the Siddhas, The Garbage and the Goddess.* However, the group is in no way governed by or accountable to Bubba Free John. He is not the present source of their theological convictions or of their ethical standards. As a matter of fact, the group differs in numerous respects from the norms established by the Free Communion Church. For example, the Surrey community is not strictly vegetarian, allows its members to smoke, and practices no regular form of meditation or spiritual exercise. Bubba remains an important and essential influence on the group but he may in no way be termed a leader of the group. In fact, the group is democratic and has no formal leader.

The Surrey community is certainly not highly structured; nor is it strictly disciplined. Decisions are reached by consensus and all disagreements are seriously considered. The group has a tendency to disparage negative responses and to demand positive attitudes. However, they do not force a member who is angry or discouraged to sublimate his or her emotional state. Rather the group confronts the individual in a loving and supportive manner until such negative moments are worked through. There is a great deal of role differentiation within the group. There is a definite sense of "men's work" and "women's work." The men are responsible for major decisions, particularly those dealing with financial matters. The "ladies" are responsible for domestic matters, such as cooking, cleaning, child rearing, etc. Each member of the group does what he or she feels the most comfortable doing, whether it is writing, painting, house cleaning, or outside employment.

Economic considerations certainly have influenced many decisions. But my primary impression is that an honest attempt is made to create opportunities for self-fulfillment despite economic and group requirements. The community is definitely communal—that is, the total resources are shared by the collective. On a day-to-day basis the control of resources is very loosely structured, with individual members rotating the function of treasurer and accountant among themselves. The group has functioned successfully for more than two years without outside financial assistance. Now and then their monthly accounts were in the red but the group managed to survive. In more recent times there has been a more substantial infusion of cash, primarily from two members of the group, Louis and Marjorie. Virtually all of the $80,000 to $100,000 currently in the group's treasury may be traced to one or other of the Browns. The community's plan is to invest these resources in real estate. As of this date, the sudden riches of the group have not been reflected in any material acquisitions. Without these funds the community would have been poorly equipped to respond to the challenge of recent events, particularly to the legal and professional costs to which they have been obligated in the aftermath of the kidnapping-deprogramming of the Netskis.

Basically the community is economically self-sufficient even without the funds of its two affluent members. The group's cooperative painting business, which involves four of the men on a full-time basis, has apparently established a reputation for excellence and is obtaining major contracts. Three or four of the women in the group are involved in a housecleaning service. Each woman works approximately two days a week and is free to pursue domestic and child-rearing responsibilities the remaining days. Plans for further economic development of the community are somewhat unrealistic, vague, and tenuous. Henry Stevens and John Howard are pursuing careers as "novelists." The community is highly supportive of their efforts and believes that they will produce "best sellers." In addition, three or four members of the group were described to me as professional musicians and plans for the production of recordings were related to me by several members of the group. It is difficult to see how such aesthetic aspirations will generate cash revenues in the foreseeable future. There is a definite sense that once bare essentials have been provided by the painting and housecleaning endeavors, it will be necessary for the group to develop other activities, not only for income but to provide opportunities for the greatest possible self-expression of each individual member.

The discipline of the group is achieved through positive reinforcement rather than through punishment or humiliation. There are some general standards of behavior but little fanaticism in the observance of norms. The group espouses vegetarianism yet eats meat, fish, and poultry on "special occasions." The group encourages a healthy diet yet allows its members to purchase "junk food" treats with communal funds. There is a certain rebelliousness and flouting of authority which prohibits the group from taking even its minimal standards of behavior too seriously. From every indication, the group is strictly monogamous and espouses a standard of sexual fidelity. On the evening of the second day of my visit the sixth and final couple in the community was legally married. Hence, the group today consists of six married couples, their four children, and one remaining single male.

I found no evidence of religious rituals, worship, meditation, group encounter sessions, drug-induced ecstasy, or therapy sessions. It would be difficult to indict the group for brainwashing, mind control, or inducing altered states of consciousness. There is some food faddishness, e.g. two fast periods a year, which might disturb the members' physical and mental equilibrium. But this is a far cry from the manipulativeness of cult organizations.

FINAL CONSIDERATION: PARENTS AND CHILDREN

The attitudes of parents in the group toward their offspring were impressive. Each child knows that he or she has a mother and a father. In addition, the entire group assumes responsibility for providing emotional support and guidance to the children. Each child receives a tremendous amount of time and attention and affection. At the same time, each is encouraged to develop resources of self-sufficiency. Children are disciplined in a direct, confrontive manner. Boundaries are clearly established and sanctions upheld with an appropriate "no" or an occasional slapped hand. A serious affront such as petty thievery could lead to the cancellation of off-ground privileges for a number of months. In sum, discipline was neither lax nor abusive.

Franny's case report, "Alleged Abuse of Noble Netski," confirms my findings. He states:

> The abduction of Bella and Thomas seemed to me to be inappropriate, ill-timed and potentially dangerous. At the time, Bella was seven months pregnant. Needless to say, an abduction of any kind is stressful, and the attempted deprogramming of Bella at such a critical time might have threatened the unborn child. Most deprogrammings are contracted by parents, who arrange the capture and restraint of their children so that the deprogramming can take place. This has provided legal validity, as many American courts have ruled that a parent cannot be convicted of kidnapping their own child. However, in this case, the Williamses had arranged not only for the capture of their daughter, but Thomas Netski, as well. His parents were not involved in or supportive of the deprogramming.

As for the allegations of child abuse which Mrs. Williams had lodged against the group, Franny set out to determine their substance by applying professionally accepted criteria of child well-being: living environment; educational resources; evidence of physical abuse, emotional maladjustment, or neglect; child's behavior with regard to normal developmental stages; individual parental attitudes and philosophy of child rearing, age and emotional history of parents; presence of stimulating/nurturing interaction with parents, other adults, or children; nutrition and physical care of the child; and how the group lifestyle or extended family affects the child.

Franny found that the physical atmosphere was "a very

healthy one for a child" and that "stimulating resources" (toys, pets, games, a garden) were "plentiful." The child was robust, healthy, mature, and verbal. There was no sign of abuse. He added: "There certainly is no evidence of failure to thrive." Franny observed that the child was well aware of who his mother and father were. He states: "Though he recognizes and trusts other adults, his primary emotional attachment is evidently for his parents." The Netskis received high marks for attentive parenting. No evidence of abusiveness was noted. However, Noble had experienced "developmental setbacks" (bed-wetting and tantrums) during the deprogramming. First, he was separated from his parents under circumstances which were deeply stressful and confusing to the child. Then he was restored to their company but discovered that they were not allowed to discipline or restrict him. By the time of our visit, the situation was back to normal.

In sum, Franny found "no evidence of abusive or neglectful behavior from his parents." Their care of him was consistent, involved, and active. There was simply no grounds for "removing him from his natural parents."

Franny agreed that the group is not a cult or an affiliate of a cult. They are, he said, a commune rather than a cult. He felt that their allegiance to BFJ was "symbolic."

The community claims no ideological exclusivity. The truths which it has gained from Bubba Free John are truths regarded as previously known and reverenced prior to all association with Bubba Free John. Further, such truths are simple and basic and may be found in any religious tradition by any sincere individual. The community is not involved in any systematic recruitment effort. New members have not been sought. They have been brought by their own curiosity and have stayed because of essential compatibilities with earlier members. However, many visitors have been discouraged from remaining more than a day or two because they were seen by the existing group as too obsessively dedicated to the pursuit of a given world view or ethical standard or dietary practice. Other than the recognition of a need to find a mate for the one single male member of the group, every member of the group expressed a feeling of contentment with the present complement of the community.

Although in many respects the group is self-contained, it does not define itself in opposition to the outside world. The group subscribes to a daily newspaper, watches television on a regular basis, attends motion pictures. Recently it was decided not to segregate children in the group from the public education system. The one child in the group who is of school age is attending kindergarten at a local public school. Relationships between members of the community and family members and friends are totally dependent on the wants and needs of each individual. It is my feeling that a great deal of alienation and tension has existed between members of the community and their respective parents. Motivations for this are diverse. Some members of the group have deliberately rejected and continue to reject attitudes, aspirations, and values of their parents. Some members of the group have retreated from domineering and controlling parents. Other members of the group regard their parents as hostile to their communal lifestyle. Some see their parents as totally indifferent. A few view their families as mildly supportive. Recent events have made the group acutely aware of the possible repercussions of misunderstandings and fouled communications. Some members are making deliberate efforts to reestablish mutually satisfying communications between themselves and their parents. Although it is clear that many familial relationships are in need of repair, it is also apparent that the community in no way encourages members to cut ties with family members or friends.

Probably the greatest source of irritation felt by parents pertains to the area of career decisions. Many of the members of the community are college-educated but none of them is actively pursuing the career for which he or she was trained. For example, Thomas Netski holds a degree in biochemistry yet works as a house painter. Cathy Stevens is a certified teacher, yet is content to spend her time in domestic duties. Clearly, group members value emotional rewards such as happiness, self-fulfillment, and satisfying interpersonal relationships while their parents are concerned with such consider-

ations as financial security and social prestige. Now we are at
the heart of the fundamental conflict which cannot be readily
reconciled. On the one side is the community with its rejection
of careerism and materialism and on the other hand we find
parents of every conceivable circumstance from working-class
immigrants to the scions of exceptional wealth united in frustration and bitterness at progeny whose aspirations fall well
below their talents and capabilities. Thus, the culture versus
counterculture debate of the past two decades continues between the members of the Surrey community and their elders.

In sum, the Surrey community is an intentional extended
family or economic commune composed of individuals who
care for one another and who are deeply committed to common goals. The group is to some extent influenced by the
writings of Bubba Free John and revere him as a teacher.
However, the community is in no way connected with the Free
Communion Church or Bubba Free John personally. The accusation voiced by Mary Williams and Ted Patrick that the
group is a cult and that its members are brainwashed is unsup-
ported, unwarranted, and malicious. Unfortunately, Dr. Williams's efforts to obtain intervention on behalf of Belinda have
not abated. While my report was being prepared she was in
contact with both Margaret Singer, Ph.D., an eminent authority on brainwashing, and my associate Joshua Baran. Mary is
still convinced that Belinda has entered a trap from which the
younger woman is unable to extricate herself. Mary also believes that a second daughter who has no involvement with the
Surrey community is an additional victim of the irresistible
mind-control techniques of the Bubba Free John cult. Mary's
search for the ideal deprogrammer goes on. Thus, as of this
writing, the war against "the cult that never was" continues.

SURPRISE ENDINGS

Surprise ending number one: No charges were ever brought
against the deprogrammers by the authorities in Clark County,

Washington. The Board of Supervisors refused to appropriate funds for prosecution, feeling that Ted Patrick has "suffered enough" through his conviction on kidnapping charges in the Roberta McElfish case. This is an outrage. For the sum of twenty thousand dollars, Patrick abducted a seven-month-pregnant woman and her husband. The mother-to-be was subjected to brutal stress, sleep deprivation, disruption of her accustomed diet, and was forced to cede custody of her son to her mother. She was told that the deprogrammers would knock down the door and forcibly remove the child and harm her friends if she did not cooperate. Her husband was kidnapped at the behest of his mother-in-law and coerced into recanting his affiliation with a group to which he did not belong. He was assaulted by Patrick during the deprogramming, his life was threatened, he was told that if he ever went back to the cult, Patrick and his henchmen would kick in the doors and kill him. The Netskis suffered the further indignity of having every moment of their deprogramming videotaped by ever-present TV cameras. When the couple pretended to be deprogrammed in order to escape the close scrutiny of the group, they were told that they would be sent to San Diego for "rehab" and that they would then have the opportunity to join the anticult crusade and assist in deprogrammings. Their son suffered emotional disturbances. For months after their traumatic ordeal, the Netskis experienced nightmares, depression, rage, and a sense of helplessness. Yet the authorities felt that Ted Patrick had "suffered enough."

Not long ago, I chanced upon Sarah Blaine who provided the condominium where the Netskis were held. Our meeting was not cordial. She screamed at me in a crowded exhibit hall: "You work for the cults. You put Ted Patrick in prison. You wrote a letter to the judge in San Diego, telling him to put Ted Patrick in jail. You don't believe in brainwashing or mind control. You don't believe that Bubba Free John is a cult." This woman had her own daughter kidnapped by Ted Patrick years ago. The young woman had married a man of whom the mother did not approve. There was not a hint of cult involvement. The deprogramming failed and Patrick was arrested. He invoked the "doctrine of necessity" or "justification" defense that has since been used successfully hundreds of times. His client believed, it was argued, that her daughter was in grave peril. The mother believed that kidnapping her daughter was the lesser of two evils. Patrick was merely the mother's agent. Since the mother was innocent under the "justification doctrine," her agent was also innocent. Having learned nothing from her courtroom experiences, that mother is part of a ring of kidnappers which continues to punish young adults like her daughter who refuse to accept their parents' authority after they have entered adulthood.

Surprise ending number two: after Patrick's conviction in the McElfish case, a probation officer from San Diego County phoned me and asked me whether I felt that Patrick's actions were required for the preservation of American civilization. I told him that I detested such inappropriate kidnappings as those of Roberta McElfish and the Netskis. When Patrick was sentenced to a year in jail and five years' probation, it was widely rumored that I was responsible—despite the fact that more than a thousand expressions of support from individuals representing every conceivable profession and position, including judges, were considered by the court. Patrick's administrative assistant phoned Franny while we were in the midst of a case, and after telling our client that I was no good and had sent Ted Patrick to prison, she demanded of Franny that he immediately resign as my employee. He did. Talk about post-hypnotic suggestions!

Surprise ending number three: Embittered and angered by the failure of law enforcement to protect them from the kidnappers as well as by the court's refusal to prosecute, the group sought reintegration into the Free Communion Church. Ironically, the president and officers of the Church came to me to seek my advice. Over the years I have found them eager to reconcile squabbling family members and to rectify any alleged injustices committed by the group. (I am probably the only cult counselor who maintains regular and fruitful liaison with the leadership of cult groups whenever possible. I always give the group the opportunity to prove to me that it lives by the standards which it espouses. I have been occasionally disappointed but often pleasantly surprised.) Knowing the background of the situation and the expected family reactions, I advised them not to readmit those who had voluntarily left the Church years ago. "If you do," I commented, "you are asking for trouble." The Church officers agreed and denied the applications of the previous members. However, they placed no obstacles in the path of Surrey commune members who had not previously been associated with the Free Communion Church.

It would seem that the members of the Surrey commune are willing to allow their minds to bend according to their peculiar bent. And this peculiar bent is in the direction of Da Free John's Free Communion Church. Nothing produces zeal like persecution. And there are few capable of persecuting young adults with the fervor of Mary Williams, Sarah Blaine, and Ted Patrick. As I review the case after the passage of nearly four years, I find evidence that the Netskis were indeed the victims of mind-bending, that is that they were subjected to a deliberate and concerted effort to throw them off balance emotionally, to induce cathartic reactions, and to alter radically their attitudes and way of life. Without question the mind-benders were not the "Bubba Free John cult" but the deprogrammers and those who hired them.

4

❧❧❧

Why Here? Why Now?

A GROUNDSWELL OF BELIEF

Why in this society and at this time are we beset by aggressive conversionist movements? The answer is twofold. First, there is and always has been something about America which predisposes us toward outbreaks of religious fervor. Second, there is something about this particular time in our history which inclines us toward specific forms of sectarianism.

A recent newspaper article reported a "ground swell of religious belief." The report states:

> Most adult Americans are more interested in religion than they were five years ago, although less than half say they actually participate in religious activities, according to a Gallup poll.
>
> The survey, conducted for the Christian Broadcasting Network, also found that Americans have a growing belief that religion can answer the problems of the world, while faith in science to solve these problems has dropped.
>
> "Religious interest and involvement is extremely high in this country and growing, but deep commitment levels are still at a fairly low level," pollster

> George Gallup told a news conference . . . at
> CBN's studios here.[1]

Gallup's findings were based on a telephone survey of 1,209
adults which was conducted July 22–31, 1983. Fifty-seven percent of those contacted said that they were currently more
interested in spiritual matters than they were five years earlier.
However, only 41 percent claimed that they had recently taken
part in religious activities other than worship services. Fifty-
four percent said that they were more likely today to believe
that religion can answer the problems of the world than they
were five years ago. Thirty-six percent said that they were
more likely to believe that science can solve the problems of
the world than they were five years ago, while 47 percent said
that they were less likely to hold that belief. No clear pattern of
explanations for any of these shifts in belief emerged.

The survey also disclosed that more than half of those questioned are "more reliant on God today than five years ago."
Eighty-five percent said they think "it is important for Americans to become more interested in religion." From these data,
Pat Robertson, the TV evangelist who is president of CBN,
concluded that there is "a profound ground swell of religious
belief in our nation."[2]

That there really is such a ground swell is certainly not
established by the survey. However, when these results are
compared with other survey-generated data, a clearer picture
emerges. In 1952, 75 percent of Americans said that religion
was "very important" in their lives. In 1965, the figure was still
a significantly high 70 percent. By 1978, the percentage had
declined to about 53—just slightly over half the population.[3]
So whether or not there is any widespread revival of religious
fervor, there probably is one of the regular readjustments of
religion and social reality to one another which constantly
characterizes the American scene. To put it in simplest terms,
the pendulum is swinging slightly to the religious right—just
as it did after World War II. It is also interesting to note that
despite the erosion of the importance of religion, both the
percentage of respondents who believed that Jesus was "God"

or "the Son of God" and the percentage who prayed were essentially identical in 1952 and 1978.[4]

Since Robertson is a principal promoter of revivalistic religion, his opinion may be dismissed as self-serving. To provide a context for understanding the significance of the 1983 survey, it is necessary to look at earlier studies, such as the 1965 Gallup poll which sought to "measure the religious beliefs and practices of American adults, and attitudes of members of the three main religious groups toward each other," as well as to determine what changes, if any, had occurred since a similar study made by Ben Gaffin and associates in 1952. Equally important were the survey of church members in northern California conducted by sociologists Charles Y. Glock and Rodney Stark in 1963 and a survey of a representative sample of the entire American adult population by National Opinion Research in 1964.[5] These surveys were far more significant and informative than the 1983 Gallup findings.

What do Americans believe? First, they believe in God. Eighty-one percent are "absolutely certain there is a God." An additional 12 percent are "fairly sure." And only 2 percent do not believe in God at all. Eighty-three percent believe in the Trinity. A striking 72 percent say that they believe that Jesus is God, while only 13 percent claim that he is "just another leader like Mohammed or Buddha." The vast majority of Americans believe that Jesus was born of a virgin, walked on water, and will actually return to earth someday.

For many years—if not for several decades—the convictions of most Americans regarding the existence of God and the person of Jesus Christ have been quite compatible with the doctrines of orthodox Christianity—i.e., there is a God; he watches over the lives of his children; he was present in the world in the person of Jesus of Nazareth; Jesus was born of a virgin, he is the divine Son of God, the worker of miracles. As for the Bible, nearly four fifths (79 percent) of the American population classify the Bible as the "revealed word of God," while only 13 percent consider it to be "only a great piece of literature." The biblical miracles were doubted or rejected by only 17 percent of the Protestants and 9 percent of the Catholics. With regard to the Bible, the majority of Americans hold convictions which are consonant with the basic doctrines of fundamentalism.

Moreover, three quarters of all Americans believe in life after death. Only 10 percent indicated that they reject the belief. Sixty-eight percent believe that there is a heaven where good people are eternally rewarded. More than half profess that they believe that there is a hell "to which people who have led bad lives and die without being sorry are eternally damned."

Salvation—"Christianity's central concern and promise"—was a focal point of the Glock-Stark research. Explored by the two sociologists were beliefs and acts considered necessary for salvation as well as improper beliefs and conduct which would be viewed as grounds for exclusion from salvation. Nearly two thirds of the Protestants and more than half the Catholics maintain that "belief in Jesus Christ as Saviour" is "absolutely necessary" for salvation. Fifty-two percent of the Protestants and 38 percent of the Catholics claim that "holding the Bible to be God's truth" is "absolutely necessary."

Concerning impediments to salvation, the majority rejected the notion that any of the following would constitute an *absolute* obstacle: not knowing about Jesus (as might be the case with persons living in another country), being Jewish, being Hindu, breaking the Sabbath, taking the name of the Lord in vain, drinking liquor, practicing birth control, discriminating against other races, or being anti-Semitic. In other words, America's pietism is softened by an element of tolerance. A finer sifting of the data shows that Protestants are divided into three religious camps: liberal, moderate, and conservative. For example, the gap between Congregationalists and Episcopalians, on the one hand, and Southern Baptists and sect members, on the other hand, on all the items in the survey is enormous. However, what we are reporting here are statistical averages.

The CBN-commissioned Gallup poll found a discrepancy between Americans' wishes that religion be more influential and their own practice. Eighty-five percent of the respondents think it is important for Americans to become more interested in religion, but only 41 percent said that they recently had taken part in religious activities other than worship services. Earlier research came to the conclusion that there exists a sizable gap between affirmations and actions. Seven out of ten Americans told Gallup that they considered religion "very important" in their lives, but less than 40 percent claimed that they attended church every week. Almost as many never attend. The combined Gallup and Glock-Stark data indicate that Americans who do attend church regularly—once a month or more—constitute a minority.

Even if we accept the church attendance figure, there are reasons for suspecting that the piety of Americans is more ceremonial than personal. Nearly four fifths of all Americans believe that the Bible is the revealed word of God, yet only one American in seven reads it "practically every day" and more than one quarter read it "never" or "practically never." Most Americans believe that religious education is important, yet only a relative handful can name the four gospels or recall three or more of the Ten Commandments. Moreover, belief in heaven and hell and the conviction that one ought to live as though one's destiny is more important than one's present life do not change the fact that nearly half of those surveyed admit that they are more serious about trying to live comfortably than preparing for an afterlife.

Selecting regular attendance at worship services and grace before meals as ritual acts which would be encouraged by all Christian groups, Glock and Stark discovered:

> In a sample of persons, all of whom were formal members of specific congregations and parishes, the Christian churches generally fail to meet the standard of universal ritual commitment; indeed the majority of Protestants and Catholics fail to fulfill even these minimal standards of ritual commitment.[6]

Since the early days of the Republic, foreign observers of the American scene have been struck by the high degree of our religious involvement as well as by the superficiality of our spiritual commitment. For as a nation we are motivated by convictions which provide us with a sense of meaning and normality. It is these convictions rather than our generally tepid church religiosity which guide and motivate our everyday lives. The content of this implicit religion was described by Will Herberg as faith in "the American Way of Life."[7] We are as a people bound together by a limited number of fundamental affirmations which transcend the claims of all other beliefs in dignity and power. The principal ingredients are: "individual freedom, personal independence, human dignity, community responsibility, social and political democracy, sincerity, restraint in outward conduct, thrift, . . . the uniqueness of the American 'order,' and the great importance assigned to religion."[8]

The attitudes of Americans are influenced by what they believe to be ultimately true, real, and desirable. One source of such convictions is the religion of their churches. A second source is civil religion, the implicit faith in the American way of life. This source borrows its symbols and its substance from two somewhat incompatible traditions: pietistic Christianity and liberal humanism. The convictions of the American liberal tradition are as follows: man is a rational being capable of solving the problems of his society through the application of reason and technology; the United States of America is based on self-evident truths (embodied in the Declaration of Independence, the Constitution, and its various institutions); and the special destiny of America is to spread these truths to all the nations of the world and to remove all obstructions to the realization of these truths. The liberal humanist heritage in no way depends on the civil religion. But there could be no American civil religion without the liberal tradition.

Alongside the creeds of the churches they attend, Americans possess a more basic set of precepts: the belief in skill, competence, efficiency, perseverance, and organization; the willingness to respond to competition; and the conviction that the United States enjoys a special destiny in the world.[9] As Herberg observes:

> If the American Way of Life had to be defined in one
> word, "democracy" would undoubtedly be the word,
> but democracy in a peculiarly American sense. On its
> political side, it means the Constitution; on its eco-
> nomic side, "free enterprise"; on its social side, an
> equalitarianism which is not only compatible with but
> indeed actually implies vigorous economic competi-
> tion and high mobility. . . .
>
> The American Way of Life is individualistic, dy-
> namic, pragmatic. It affirms the supreme value and
> dignity of the individual; it stresses incessant activity
> on his part . . . ; defines an ethic of self-reliance,
> merit, and character; and judges by achievement.
> . . . The American Way of Life is humanitarian, "for-
> ward looking," optimistic. . . . The American be-
> lieves in progress, in self-improvement, and quite fa-
> natically in education. But above all, the American is
> idealistic. . . . And because they are so idealistic,
> Americans tend to be moralistic; they are inclined to
> see all issues as plain and simple, black and white,
> issues of morality.[10]

As a nation, we are bound to faith in the American way of life.
We see ourselves as a unique and superior society ordained
and protected by God. Religious institutions have an important role to play in the promulgation of this faith, for they
sanctify our aims, ideals, and standards. And because the
churches proclaim, defend, apply, and legitimate the American way of life—because the churches are the first and most
vehement accusers of all who deviate from our implicit faith—
Americans grant to religion a place of honor and dignity
shared by no other social institution. To put it simply, we
believe in religion.

REVIVALISM AND HUMANISM

Americans respond favorably and habitually to principles drawn from at least four diverse sources: (a) revivalistic Christianity with its emphasis upon man's sinful nature and the need for divine intervention in human affairs; (b) an optimistic and messianic commitment to the American way of life; (c) a progressive, rationalistic spirit of dedication to the solution of social problems through the manipulation of social structures (which is usually designated "liberalism"); and (d) a distrust of centralized government and a commitment to rugged individualism, laissez-faire economics, and the work ethic.

There is incredible tension between the four traditions. At the present time, we witness the fundamentalist "Moral Majority" attack upon "liberal humanism," which is in many ways a replay of the fundamentalism-modernism and creationism-evolutionism squabbles of fifty to eighty years ago. The Moral Majority believes that it is restoring America to its "Christian heritage." Its attempt to impose a partisan and reactionary version of the American way upon the nation completely overlooks the fact that the ideological foundations of the nation are more ethical-humanistic than they are revivalistic. It was from an imposed theocratic state, with its unyielding theology and morality, as well as from the wars spawned by ideological intolerance that the progenitors of this nation fled. (To be sure, it did not take some of them long to create intolerant little theocracies of their own—all of which eventually crumbled before the onslaught of humanistic tolerance.)

Just as the tension between revivalism and humanism has been exacerbated in recent years, so has the ongoing struggle between social interventionists (liberals, black activists, women's libbers, gay rights advocates, etc.) and the conservative defenders of the status quo. Nearly a half century of one-party rule by the Democratic coalition of minorities, big-city machines, unionists, Southern reactionaries, and structural tinkerers has given way to a government committed little to redressing grievances or redistributing wealth and more to the shoring up of older social, ethical, economic, and political certainties. In sum, we are in the midst of an attempt to recover the sense that "what is good for General Motors is good for the nation" at a time when General Motors (together with many other smokestack industries, farming, the airlines, banking, and education) cannot discern what is "good for General Motors."

The content of our common faith is well detailed by Will Herberg. He reminds us of our common faith in individualism, self-reliance, humanitarianism, optimism, and self-improvement. The means for attaining the goals of our faith may be expressed in one phrase: success through personal achievement.[11] For the belief that the individual can improve himself and contribute to the betterment of his society is the foundation stone of our common faith. It is when this conviction is undermined that the balance between revivalism and humanism is upset.

As a general rule, fundamentalism flourishes, not when things are bad, but when it appears that they could get appreciably worse. Humanism and political liberalism flourish, not when things are going well, but when it appears that they are going to get much better. For generations Americans cherished the hope that their lives would be better than their parents' and that their children's lives would be better yet. Such expectations died during the turmoil of the 1970s. The Arab oil embargo, the retreat from Vietnam, runaway inflation, high unemployment, the resignation of a disgraced President and Vice-President, combined with racial tensions, the disappearance of many traditional male-female role distinctions, the destabilization of the family, and the loosening of sexual morality, dealt a savage blow to our confidence in ourselves. Catastrophe breeds courage, but the constant threat of catastrophe brings despair. Change can be invigorating, but constant change produces uncertainty, disillusionment, and cynicism. Anything which promises certainty, hope, and simple remedies for complex personal and social problems becomes enormously attractive.

When a society rejects the way things have been done in the past but cannot find acceptable directions for the future, authoritarianism exerts its greatest appeal. It is not magical technologies of mind control which account for the relative success of today's fringe religious phenomena. What is remarkable is that they have not been even more successful in winning converts and attaining a position of power and influence. For most of them express our pervasive but shallow beliefs in God, Jesus, and the Bible; articulate our despair as citizens of a society so often out of control; give voice to our guilt as selfish beings unwilling to keep our word or honor our commitments; and provide promises of a better world, which is soon to come.

WHAT AMERICANS BELIEVE

Whatever else cults and sects may be, they are surely orthodox manifestations of all that we as Americans believe. Do we believe that success may be attained through hard work, dedication, and inspiration? So do they. Do we believe that momentary gratification should be postponed for the sake of greater goals? So do they. Do we believe that it is wrong to dull our senses with alcohol and opiates? So do they. Do we honor and respect the family as the building block of society and the guardian of its accumulated wisdom? They do too. Do we profess that it is important to read the Bible, pray, attend worship services, and devote ourselves to the religious education of our families? What cult or sect would disagree?

Is it not ironic that we, for the most part, honor our convictions through their nonobservance while members of totalistic and totalitarian groups honor them by performing them dutifully? Is there not an inherent weakness in faulting those whose ends offend us for maintaining standards of piety and morality to which we mostly give lip service? And when we look at the sins which we attribute to them, are we not describing our own?

Cults and sects do not spring forth from the forehead of Zeus full-grown and armed. They are the products of America's inability to live without faith. As has been noted, we believe in God. We believe in Jesus. We believe in the Bible. We believe in religion. Even more fundamentally, we believe in believing. Believing—i.e., being confident and courageous, being positive, having a dream and pursuing it—is central to the American Way of Life. A clear example of our faith fixation is the vast retail establishment whose very name is derived from "the American Way," the Amway Corporation. It is surely not the monetary success of average Amway distributors which fuels their ardor. For while a few distributors earn enormous sums, the rank and file typically operate at a net loss. Yet they have a dream of wealth that keeps them going.

Above all, Americans respect courage which disregards the odds, the "experts," and common sense. Terminal illness, it is believed, can be cured by vitamins, diet, attitude, or laughter. Anyone can become a millionaire by starting a business from scratch or buying a winning lottery ticket or by suing the bastards. And if faith breaks down and we fail, there is an alternate set of beliefs which gets us off the hook. The fault lies not in ourselves but in our stars, our biorhythms, our allergies, the system, politics, our diminished capacity, stress, hypoglycemia, and negative self-image. In no way is the individual accountable or responsible. For if we believe that we have been favored by God in the guise of luck, chance, and good fortune, we must also believe that tragedy, failure, and misfortune are visited upon us by some equally mysterious, transcendental force.

I would estimate that two thirds of all Americans believe in astrology—that the individual's destiny is strongly influenced, if not wholly determined, by the date and time of his birth. No belief is more open to empirical confirmation or disconfirmation. Take any date within the last fifty years. Collect biographical data on any fifty persons born on that date. Select a second date which falls under another sign of the zodiac. Compare and contrast the two groups. There either are definite similarities between those born on the same date or there are not. There definitely are major general differences between the first and the second group or there are not. Why are such tests not routinely undertaken? Because no one wants the facts. The will to believe is too overwhelming. The need to preserve a transcendental justification, a cop-out which excuses our lack of control over that which we cannot or will not control is too powerful.

Likewise I would estimate that the majority of Americans believe in psychic powers—that certain "gifted" persons can predict the future or locate a missing person or discover the burial site of a murder victim. According to my observations, such magic works in one instance per thousand. Sheer coincidence is a surer guide than any psychic. But who wants to face this reality? The few dramatic successes of psychics receive abundant media coverage, but the thousands upon thousands of failures are ignored. Every January the tabloids are filled with predictions for the new year made by America's most celebrated prognosticators. Their batting average is virtually nil. They not only predict events which do not occur but they fail to predict the most significant events which do. A few years ago, none of the tabloid-accredited sages foresaw the assassination attempts on Pope John Paul II or Ronald Reagan. Considering the abysmal failure of these sages, why do such stories appear year after year?

We want to believe. In something. In someone. In anything. Millions of us are conversions waiting to happen.

CONVERTS: TODAY AND TOMORROW

During the sixties and the seventies, my typical subject was a recent college graduate, a professional or graduate school student, or a dropout from academic life. In the eighties, blue-collar and white-collar workers and parents of young children began occupying a significant portion of my counseling schedule. At the present time, college and university campuses remain prime targets of cult and sect recruiting. Missionaries for various authoritarian groups are proceeding under assumptions which, I believe, will prove to be fallacious. Cults and sects have made minor inroads on campus during the past two decades, but that may prove to be history. To explain why the success rate of such recruiters increased in the sixties and seventies and will probably decrease in the eighties and nineties, a few observations are required.

To generalize, young adults of the 1950s wanted to fit in, to adjust, to be accepted, to succeed. For them a college education was a passport to a good-paying job, a house in the suburbs, and the respect of one's neighbors. The college student of the fifties could conform to the standards imposed upon him by society because he could accept the viability of that society. And there was ample room for him in that society—unless he was black or a beatnik or a Communist. The student of the sixties would not commit himself to the cozy assumptions of the previous generation. The sixties brought a generation of noisy dissidents bent upon avoiding the unquestioning conformity of the student of the fifties. Every generation of young adults has questioned the values of their elders, but the college students of the sixties were more than critics of the status quo. For the Vietnam War provided a focus for several minor social revolutions. And energies that previously had fueled only the acceptable, harmless pranks of youth now were directed against the established order. Vietnam not only divided this nation but encouraged every dissenter, whatever his or her cause, to challenge the system that had tolerated and countenanced the moral muddle of American foreign policy. Conflict over the war in Asia created a climate of assault upon every social convention.

Traditional sexual morality was attacked as repressive. Accustomed sexual roles were seen as inequitable and exploitative. Prohibitions on the use of such substances as marijuana and LSD were flouted (sometimes with reasoned appeals, more often with utter disregard for the need to reason at all). Still there was ample room in the economy and, somehow, each side was able to accommodate the other. And besides, the rebels were never more than a minority—a highly visible, discordant, and all too influential minority in the eyes of the media perhaps, but a minority nonetheless.

The present college generation lives with a realization that sets them apart from those who have gone before them. There is no longer ample room. At least half those who received college degrees in the seventies as well as those about to receive them in the eighties will experience the spirit-crushing humiliation of finding themselves a surplus commodity. Education no longer guarantees upward mobility. It does not even guarantee a job. The vast majority of college graduates are employed in positions that only a few years ago were the domain of those without college degrees. According to the United States Department of Labor, by the time this book is published all professions—including medicine—may well be stocked to the brim.[12]

The students in my classes in the early sixties were fascinating. They were experimenters, advocates, adversaries, and idealists. The students of the late sixties were frustrating. They expected immediate gratification of every need, instant redress for every grievance (real or imagined), the maximum return for the least possible effort. But my dealings with the college students of the seventies conjure up one mood more than any other—depression.

They were frequently depressed, and as a teacher I often became depressed myself by the lack of enthusiasm, unwillingness to work, and decreased abilities of my students. By 1970, the basic student skills of reading, writing, and computation could no longer be presupposed. Grades had been devalued during the Vietnam War, when academic failure could cancel a student's draft deferment. Entrance standards were down in the name of greater opportunity for disadvantaged youths. Hard work and discipline were passé. And word was getting around that there were few jobs. Glum prospects produced withdrawn, despondent students who received little public attention. "Insecurity," notes Joel Kotkin, "has produced a deep, internalized despair among young people. Such numbing emotions are not likely to be picked up by the news media because pervasive depression is not usually very expressive."[13]

In some ways, the campuses of the eighties seem to have come back to the mood of the fifties. The word is: "Stay cool. Don't get involved. Don't mess up; you are going to have a hard enough time getting a job." While the typical student of the fifties was willing to play by the rules of middle America, the student of the eighties tends to find those rules unworkable. The rejection of middle-class standards of behavior that characterized the rebels of a few years ago is still a fixture of the youth culture. But the vision of anything resembling an alternative lifestyle has not yet emerged. Most young people want the security of middle-class existence, but they have none of the attitudes, values, or standards upon which such a way of life is based. In the words of one critic, Joseph Bell: "Today's young people . . . are bereft of either the passions and causes of the '6o's or the self-discipline and internal restraints built into young Americans of earlier generations."[14]

Lack of restraint and career orientation are a poor mix. In the eyes of today's young adult (and many of his elders), traditional sources of leadership and authority cannot be trusted. But no new ones have come along to take their place. It is a difficult time to become an adult, and not an easy time to be one. At no time since the Great Depression have the pre-adult years been so excruciatingly painful. No longer children and not yet adults, young people must endure confusion and anxiety. Dissatisfied with their state and powerless to change it, they direct their frustrated anger at their parents and all adult-controlled institutions. Some try to change the society against which they harbor such resentment. Others stubbornly hang on, expressing their disenchantment with abundant cynicism. A few reject that society as beyond redemption, choosing to drop out and seek some private salvation through drugs, violence, Oriental philosophy, or life in a rural commune. Some adopt what psychiatrist Erik Erikson terms "a negative identity," rejecting everything that their parents taught them to value and valuing everything their parents taught them to reject. Most flow from one immediate satisfaction to the next with no fixed direction or goal. And many become converts!

Why does an individual join a cult or sect? To escape self-dissatisfaction, loneliness, and boredom. When is an individual most susceptible to the lure of a religious movement? When he is unhappy with himself; when the demands upon him seem too great and his resources too meager; when the future seems murky, and all that appears ahead in the tunnel is more tunnel.

What leads one toward religious conversion? In the past, individuals and societies have been most susceptible to religious experience during periods of scarcity, uncertainty, hopelessness, and boredom. When there is great want and frustration, men and women will turn to powers greater than themselves for aid and comfort. When established values break down and the future appears threatening, they will likewise turn away from all that they associate with suffering and anxiety and turn toward anyone or anything that seems to offer a way of escape.

The young adults whose conversion experiences I have studied knew little of deprivation. They were well housed, well fed, well clothed by their elders. It was not a sense of material insecurity that led them to seek beyond the mundane world. They suffered a terrible emptiness—a lack, not of the necessities of life, but of the values that make life human, humane, and fulfilling. Above all, they were motivated to seek personal salvation by an overwhelming sense of boredom and loneliness. After all, when life is an endless struggle for survival no one is ever bored. When men and women are united in a life-and-death conflict as they were during World War II, who is lonely?

Is their need real or neurotic? Are the satisfactions they seek essential or illusory? Are they saints or spoiled brats? Prophets of a better way or self-indulgent dilettantes? Do they provide alternative lifestyles or temporary entertainment? Even if we cannot accept them at face value, we owe them more than our skeptical, out-of-hand rejection. Can we really offer them a more engaging, challenging, and fulfilling way of life than the alternatives provided by the cults? Can our society offer it to us?

For young adults are not the only cult-prone members of our society. The last ten years have seen disruptions which have undermined the faith of the middle-aged and the elderly in the viability of middle-class mores and assumptions. Basic realignments in the nature of our economy have thrust career blue-collar and white-collar workers onto the unemployment rolls. Forced early retirement of executives in many fields, the demobilization of Vietnam War era officers and NCOs, the decline of "bread basket" industries such as steel manufacturing and automobile assembly, have done much more than increase the statistical indices of joblessness. They have accelerated the loss of self-confidence and pessimism of the "average" citizen. They have destroyed trust in the free marketplace and the government as pillars of the status quo. They have sown the seeds of resentment, frustration, and fear throughout the society. A nation with one third of all employable males of age fifty and older out of work, with massive unemployment of minorities and vast underemployment of the skilled and educated, is a society at risk. The narcissistic psychological deprivations of the last two decades are giving way to some distressing real deprivations in the 1980s and beyond. Such is the stuff of which social upheavals and religious revivals are made. I would predict that the problems of a relative handful of middle-class families whose post-adolescent sons and daughters have been caught up in a few relatively tiny religious groups will be as nothing compared to the fanaticism and extremism of the next twenty years.

And will this abundant crop of converts be Moonies, Hare Krishnas, Children of God, Divine Light Mission followers, or Scientologists? Probably not. The major missionary inroads of the eighties through the end of the century will be made by ultrafundamentalist sects—extreme offshoots of independent fundamentalist churches and Pentecostalism. At Freedom Counseling Center, cases involving such groups have already replaced the cults spotlighted by the Anticult Network. The religious experience and theologies of the ultrafundamentalist sects are based on healing, speaking in tongues, and deliverance. Their expectations for our society are pessimistic and grim. Their polity is pyramidal and authoritarian. And their growth is rapid.

In a sense, such sects are much more familiar to America than the imported cults from the Orient and the heretical offshoots of Christendom. The ultrafundamentalist sects are biblical, trinitarian, and millenarian. Americans are comfortable with reverence for the Bible and theological orthodoxy. Dispensational fundamentalism, with its anticipation of the imminent return of Jesus, has flourished in this country for a century. Using the dispensational fundamentalist interpretation of the Bible as a point of departure and then building one's own idiosyncratic sect is like buying a franchise. Initially, the new group benefits by its similarity to an established and relatively noncontroversial stance. Recruits with no previous knowledge of the Bible are impressed with the way the founder-prophet's system fits together so well. And converts from established dispensationalist groups are impressed with the continuity between old and new allegiances, and fascinated by the innovative (and obviously superior) teachings of the new.

The "hottest" prospects for the near future are experiential groups which emphasize gifts of the spirit: tongues, healing, prophecy, and deliverance.[15] In such groups, evil spirits are regarded as the cause of all negative human experiences, such as sickness, anger, strife, crime, and war. Illness is "cured" by the laying on of hands and exorcism of evil spirits. Medicine is strongly opposed. Government in such groups is strict and authoritarian, demanding total submission to leadership. Members are often instructed to lie, steal, defraud, abandon marriages and careers. Refusal to obey a leader's instructions is considered rebellion against God. Leaders are accorded special privileges and are not bound by the laws of man or even by biblical injunctions. For they claim to be God's only apostle of the last days, God's only true prophet, or Jesus Christ returned.

Most groups are communal, maintaining only minimal contact with the outside world. Possessions, real estate, and financial resources are "held in common," which in practice means that they are controlled by the group leadership. Marriages are arranged; children are frequently viewed as the property of the collective. Child abuse and neglect are rampant in such groups. Romantic love and parental concern for children are often condemned as "idolatry."

Why do such groups abound? They suit the times. They provide myths which interpret present conditions. They explain our sense of futility in the face of our overwhelming problems—personal, social, national, and international. They articulate our fear of technology and our distrust of medicine. They satisfy our fantasies of finding love by placating an angry parent. They grant us identity and a sense of belonging. They entertain and distract. They give us authority in which we can trust. They simplify our lives by reducing them to the ongoing struggle between God and Satan, thereby allowing us to reject the notion that we are responsible for our lives and destinies. They take away our anxieties at the cost of our freedom.

5

❦❦❦❦

The Dangers of
Cults and Sects

Although I am opposed to vigilante efforts to kidnap cult and sect members in order to forcibly deconvert them, this does not mean that I find such groups harmless. Far from it. For I am well aware of behavior within cults and sects which is psychologically devastating, morally repugnant, and socially unacceptable. Fanaticism, with its "the ends justify the means" morality, its willingness to sacrifice the individual for the sake of group goals, its opposition to reason, remains today what it has been at all times in human history—an enormous force for evil.

Much of the harm done by cults and sects is intrinsic to their nature. Too many groups with which I deal are dictatorships. The frustrations and uncertainties of democratic decision-making processes have been transcended. There is no room for self in authoritarian groups. There is intensity and identity for the submissive and only for the submissive. There is little opportunity for rational inquiry, personal growth, or creative thinking.

THE POWER OF GROUPS

Groups cause harm. Michael D. Langone, Director of Research at the American Family Foundation has set forth a hierarchy of propositions about groups, the response to which categorizes the respondent as procult or anticult in orientation. I would like to use these statements in a somewhat different manner, to make a general statement about the "dangers" of groups as follows:

1. Groups can influence a person's behavior.

2. Groups can exploit an individual by using manipulative techniques to induce the person to do things that are in the group's rather than (and sometimes contrary to) the individual's interest.

3. Groups can harm individuals—often, but not necessarily, as a result of manipulation.

4. Manipulation, group-centered goals, and harm are dimensional, rather than categorical concepts. [Manipulation and harm happen now and then, under certain circumstances, but not at all times and in all places.]

5. Nearly all groups exploit and/or harm their members at least a little at least some of the time.

6. Because exploitation and harm are dimensional concepts, some groups may exploit and/or harm their members *more* (more intensely and/or more frequently) than is socially/ethically acceptable.

7. Some cults exploit and/or harm their members more than is socially/ethically acceptable.

8. Certain factors within individuals—e.g., unassertiveness, alienation, gullibility, spiritual searching—may render them unusually susceptible to manipulation and harm.

9. Society should do something about groups (including cults) which exploit and/or harm members more than is socially/ethically acceptable.[1]

In sum, individuals can get hurt in groups. Some people are more prone to get hurt than others. Some groups go too far. Something should be done about it.

I do not disagree with the contention that the dynamics of cults and sects tend to cause harm to the psychological and social well-being of their members. As relatively totalistic subcultures, cults and sects achieve a high degree of milieu and information control. By severely limiting the input, groups attempt to control the output—attitudes, thoughts, behavior, and activities. As Alan W. Scheflin and Edward M. Opton, Jr., have observed: "Whoever controls what there is to think about, controls what will be thought about it."[2]

The power of authoritarian groups to pattern, reparent, and resocialize is impressive. I have often been asked to explain how cults and sects are able to achieve such "sudden personality changes" in such relatively short periods of time. I have noted that they first change behavior, that changes in behavior elicit changes in attitudes, that changes in attitudes produce changes in beliefs, and, finally, changes in beliefs lead to changes in feelings. I am sure that the reader will recognize that such procedures are consistent with the motivational techniques present in many different human experiences. This process is neither original nor remarkable when used by cults and sects. What is remarkable is that so many observers find it remarkable.

ARTIFICIAL ATMOSPHERE

The process of changing behavior, attitudes, beliefs, and feelings is more likely to be achieved if there is a structured plan and an atmosphere designed for this purpose. The elements of such an "artificial atmosphere" include:

1. Seclusion—removing the subject from all distractions.

2. Instant intimacy and hierarchy—breaking down barriers through attention, affection, and approval; encouraging subjects to act silly and childish so that they will regress to a state

of childlike dependence upon the adult figures within the group.

3. Instant community—appealing to global generalities which no one will dispute as a basis for unity, e.g., we are here because we all want to be better, more loving, more effective human beings.

4. Guilt induction—exaggerating the negative aspects of life in general and encouraging the confession by the subject of his failures in particular.

5. Sensory overload—bombarding the subject with activities such as singing, exercising, sharing his feelings, participating in discussion groups, taking notes at lectures, working at chores; crowding in upon him, insisting that he communicate every feeling, depriving him of both mental and physical privacy.

6. Indoctrination—repeated presentations of an organized, outlined, and dovetailed body of new data with ample testimonies from group members that "it all fits together so well!" This is extremely impressive to those who have no sense of articulated purpose or meaning for themselves or the world in which they live. (Of course, it is less impressive to anyone who has ever presented a diverse body of material in a coherent manner by writing a dissertation, sermon, book, plan for an advertising campaign, or who has been responsible for a major social function. Things fit together because they are planned that way.)

7. Appeals to "holy" or "wise" authorities—the Bible, other sacred writings such as the Koran or the Bhagavad-Gita, big names from any field (philosophers, educators, politicians, scientists, novels, movies, or comic strips).

8. Personal testimonies of earlier converts—tearful renditions of how low the sinner had sunk (or of how high he had risen and how miserable he was anyway) accompanied by appropriate group expressions of sympathy: "I once was lost but now am found; was blind but now I see." This technique is extremely effective when persons with some claim to fame (former rock stars, beauty queens, television or movie celebri-

ties, criminals, political figures) offer their personal witness or simply lend credence to the proceedings by being present. \

9. Patterns of behavior—involvement of the potential recruit in new ways of eating, sleeping, speaking, dressing, wearing his hair, tying his shoes, burying the garbage, praying, reading the Bible, singing, greeting peers, etc. The particulars are unimportant as long as they are different. For if behavior is changed, attitudes, beliefs, and feelings will follow.

10. Social definition of reality—the conformist's implicit credo: "I like you because you like me. Because I like you, I will do as you do, feel as you feel, believe as you believe, love as you love, and hate as you hate—otherwise you will stop liking me." By taking advantage of the conformist's vulnerability, the manipulative group is able to reshape his reality.

11. Commitment by default—the initiate is not encouraged to make a conscious decision to stay; rather it is made convenient for him to stay and difficult for him to leave.

12. Contrast identity—picturing the outside world as completely evil and the group as completely good; encouraging the disruption of all ties with the outside world—family, friends, the media, and work associates.

13. Avoidance of negativity—discouraging independent or critical thought by characterizing it as negative, selfish, or disruptive.

14. Encouragement of positivity—constant stressing that the group's beliefs and practices "work," produce "gains," create happiness and peace of mind, bestow virtue, heal, etc.; praising those who conform as "spiritual," "loving," and "wise."

15. Actionizing—putting faith into action; as soon as possible having the initiate recruit, raise funds, assist in the indoctrination; overwhelming natural reticence by implicating the recruit in the group's manipulation of new marks.

16. Bombastic redescription of the familiar—"loading the language," introducing new terminology which has no meaning outside the group and redefining all familiar words by giving them new meanings (e.g., "caring" comes to mean taking advantage of another person "for his own good"; "sharing

the love of God" now means engaging in prostitution; "allowing God to bless others" means tricking them into giving money to the group by lying to them; "following the will of God" means doing whatever you want to do; and so forth. Cults redefine each act so that it is not merely eating, drinking, sleeping, earning money, etc., but a means of expressing a higher purpose and a manifestation of personal growth. The more completely the new language is taught, the more thoroughly acculturated to the group and alienated from family and friends does the convert become.

These sixteen steps are the formula for evoking sudden conversion. They are used by numerous groups—each with its own special emphasis and ideology. They are not so much a "technology of mind control" or hallmarks of brainwashing as they are a description of common techniques by which groups break down personal resistance and establish their influence. Such techniques may be used for or against our better interests. And their power is no greater than the source from which it flows—the consent of the governed. The desire of the subject to be dominated rather than the manipulative skill of the leader accounts for much of the harm suffered by the subject. No one joining a cult knows fully what he is getting himself into. But what couple exchanging wedding vows has entered into marriage with full capacity, informed consent? No matter how carefully the cult conceals its true identity during the initial indoctrination stage, no one is so naïve that he does not know that he is surrendering himself to the will of his new peers in exchange for comfort, security, and acceptance. The luring process is too obvious—even if the programmed outcome is not. The recruit willingly suppresses his inner alarm, those feelings of discomfort and apprehension which constantly sound regardless of what games the recruiter plays. For no powerfully attractive experience is without a component of dread. Intense new experiences always confront us as fascinating and terrifying mysteries. It is possible for an individual to enter a trap from which it is difficult to extract himself—but entering is a decision and a free act, as is remaining when the teeth of the trap painfully take hold.

The pain of losing control over one's life is very real—even if such loss is devoutly sought. There is always the distressing gap between the cult identity and primordial self-image. The old nature is never entirely rooted out no matter how rigorously the convert subjects himself to self-mortification, good works, prayer, study, chanting, meditation, speaking in tongues, etc. *The chattering voice of enduring selfhood cannot be silenced. But it certainly can be muffled.* Sensory deprivation or overstimulation, centering or attention-focusing techniques, excessive activity, and sleep deprivation are effective tools for silencing doubt, alienating the convert from his pre-cult existence, and effecting personality changes.

Cults and sects have a tendency to overemphasize immersion in consciousness-altering practices such as meditation, chanting, speaking in tongues, and other repetitious rituals. The convert's desire is to deepen his spiritual life, while the interest of the group is to reinforce group solidarity and denigrate individuality. This often leads to the "too much of a good thing" problem. For instance, meditation has documented therapeutic value. Twenty to forty minutes of Transcendental Meditation, reciting one's mantra or the sacred syllable "Om," concentrating on one's breathing, repeating the Lord's Prayer, or chanting "Coca-Cola" can increase a person's well being. Such practices can reduce the frequency and severity of anxiety attacks, insomnia, allergic reactions, asthma, etc. But four hours or more daily of similar activities causes the mind to lose its normal frame of reference, become dissolved in its own residue (memories, imaginings, unresolved traumas, unfulfilled wishes, and delusions), and malfunction.

"MISUSE OF MEDITATION"

A serious proponent of the therapeutic use of meditation, Patricia Carrington, Ph.D., a clinical psychologist and re-

searcher, has warned of the "misuse of meditation." She
states:

> . . . tension-release during ordinary meditation can
> produce side effects which, at times, can make for
> difficulty if they are not regulated. If meditation is
> prolonged for a matter of hours this process of ten-
> sion-release is magnified many times. When a person
> spends this much time meditating, powerful emo-
> tions and "primary process" (bizarre) thoughts may
> be released too rapidly to assimilate and the medita-
> tor may be forced into sudden confrontation with
> previously repressed aspects of him[self] . . . for
> which he is not prepared. If he has a strong enough
> ego, or is doing the extra meditation under the super-
> vision of an experienced teacher, he may weather
> such an upsurge of unconscious material and emerge
> triumphant. If he has a less strong ego or has a past
> history of emotional disturbance, he may be over-
> whelmed by it, fragile defenses may break down, and
> an episode of mental illness occur.[3]

Among my clients/subjects, I have discovered that such misuse of meditating, speaking in tongues, praying, centering
one's thoughts, reciting Bible passages, etc., is the manifestation of what may be termed an "addictive personality." Such
persons suffer from negative self-image, acute susceptibility to
peer pressure, limited impulse control, preoccupation with the
experiences of the moment, and inability to plan for the future. The addictive personality thrives on constant surges of
intensity (getting high) and drifts inexorably into relationships
of extreme dependency.

The spiritual-experience abuser approaches meditation (or
prayer, glossolalia, et al.) as though it were a new drug. The
addiction which develops is quite similar. Feelings of tranquil-
lity and ecstasy are attained through the new experience.
These feelings soon give way to a sense of emptiness. More
time, energy, and personal resources are devoted to the new
experience. Four hours a day of the new experience become

six hours as the charm of the new high wears off. Life revolves around the new state. The addict talks about little else, associates mostly with fellow addicts, becomes obsessed with maintaining the intensity level of the new experience, and loses touch with reality outside of the world of the new experience. But the emptiness returns. The addict becomes frantic. He blames himself ("I'm not dedicated enough," "I'm not adept enough"). He blames his spiritual guru or guide and finds another. He blames the distractions of the everyday world (his spouse, children, friends, job, hobbies, sex life, etc.) and withdraws from them. A cycle of emptiness, ecstasy through dedication, setback, renewal of ecstasy through greater dedication, return to the emotional slump, and so on, will continue until the subject tires of the merry-go-round and gets off, achieves an inner state which balances the ecstatic and the everyday, or becomes totally dissolved in his ecstatic states.

When existence is submersion in undifferentiated spiritual reality, the self in all of its manifestations and the world in all of its forms become ephemeral and unreal. Body, mind, other selves, nature, and society cease to be. Whether such persons are mystics and saints or psychotics and lunatics, they are no longer of this world, which is evidenced by their inability to cope with basic needs such as food, shelter, and clothing. Spiritual addiction is dangerous to one's health. Like alcoholism and drug addiction, spiritual addiction produces its share of derelicts.

How common is spiritual overdosing? How responsible is the individual? What is the role of the group? There are many organized groups which encourage the pattern of addiction which we have just described. There are numerous individuals who use such patterns to deliberately destroy their intellects and their capacity for coping. Yet the tranced-out zombie is a rarity even in such groups. There seems to be a mechanism at work which protects us from ourselves. I call it "phasing." With few exceptions, our consciousness is never at one place at one time. No matter how much we focus and concentrate, elements of inattention thwart our efforts. In our culture, the most intense spiritual states are clusters of voluntary and involuntary responses. In addition, profound experiences affect us at various levels of our being—conscious as well as unconscious. For example, glossolalia combines involuntary motor activity (inarticulate speech accompanied by jumping, rocking, arm lifting, trembling, and shaking) with an acutely focused awareness. The subject is thus simultaneously in control and out of control. His personality is engaged on conscious and unconscious levels. In a more "primitive" culture, where the ego is less developed and differentiated, loss of control would be more complete and would likely be accompanied by loss of consciousness during the trance state and would produce subsequent amnesia. The Westerner, conditioned by his culture and his social role, seldom loses control. "Role" is the key word. The individual seldom loses control even when he is assuming a new role—an "out-of-control role."

The recruit acts as the group expects him to act; acts like established members of the group who are presented to him as role models; and acts as though he has internalized the beliefs and attitudes of the group. Manipulative groups provide the role models and encourage the role-playing because they believe that attitudes adjust to behavior. They are right in this regard, for as Leon Festinger has demonstrated in his research on "cognitive dissonance," when a person's attitudes and behavior are at variance, the individual is more likely to change his attitudes to conform to his behavior than to change his behavior to be consistent with his attitudes.[4] In other words, the theory on which much cult/sect recruitment is based is: teach Eliza Doolittle to speak like royalty and she becomes royalty. But that is not the whole truth. Eliza became an altered and transformed Eliza—neither the child of the gutter with a high-society accent nor a completely different person. In rare and extreme cases, the spiritual role-player loses himself. Eliza could have ended up believing that she was Henry Higgins or that she did not exist at all. However, the vast majority of spiritual voyagers retain the ability to return home. If it were not so, who would teach the next round of converts how to meditate, chant, pray, or speak in tongues?

Since I have interviewed hundreds of cult and sect members,

it no longer amazes me when an individual steps out of his tranced-out, spacy, jargon-spouting role and speaks to me in my own language. I have come to expect it. The most acculturated cultist is able to speak my language, to beam himself aboard my sociopsychological spacecraft, as it were. Sometimes adopting the non-cult role is effortless and sometimes it sounds as though the cultist is speaking through an interpreter. And, conversely, it chills and horrifies me when the subject is unable to make the effort.

Much cult recruitment and indoctrination consists of intense, stress-inducing, group-coercive, psychologically engineered "experiments" which are designed to alter the subject's perspective, confuse his sense of identity, and render him suggestible. Such manipulation can unwittingly evoke monsters from the deep. When latent psychoses surface and are acted out, just how responsible are those who conduct such experiments? My files overflow with cases of groups encouraging the subject to surrender control and then recoiling in horror at the acts which ensued. When the genie refuses to return to the bottle, who is to blame? The cults and sects have a multitude of scapegoats: evil spirits, bad karma, unfortunate ancestors, pre-conversion brain damage, the effects of drug use, abusive parents, and guilt. Since no one can predict what will happen when a psychologically troubled individual encounters any stress, it is nearly impossible to assess the responsibility of cults and sects when their converts stumble over the edge. What is clear is that it is their purpose and intention to destabilize and reprogram. If their arrogant negligence contributes to personal tragedies, it is not unreasonable to hold them culpable.

Cults encourage attitudes and behavior which may trigger unanticipated psychotic reactions in a small percentage of their recruits. Graduate or professional school students run an equivalent risk. Although I know of no formal study of statistical comparisons, I would wager that the results would indicate that the number per thousand of law students, medical students, and liberal arts doctoral candidates who commit suicide or murder or who require hospitalization for mental illness would not be significantly different from the number per thousand of cult and sect members who commit suicide or murder or who require hospitalization for mental illness. However, in the case of professional training, society approves of the goals, purposes, and techniques of the institution and, hence, tolerates the risk. When it comes to religious groups, society is ambivalent about the goals and purposes, suspicious of the techniques, and uncomfortable with the risks. Such situations always cause public nervousness, a sense that "something ought to be done." Inevitably remedial action ensues in the form of restrictive legislation, licensing, assessing of punitive damages, closer scrutiny, or official interference. *Just as the possibility of harm is the price which society pays for its tolerance of intensity-inducing groups, so also accountability is the price of the cult or sect group's freedom of expression.*

PERMITTING THE IMPERMISSIBLE

Even when cult and sect groups cause no overt psychological harm, there are more subtle complications. *Groups define reality; and they permit the impermissible.* The power of groups to influence judgment and perception at the most basic level was demonstrated in a classic experiment by Solomon Asch. Groups of seven to nine "subjects" were assembled in a room and shown a series of cards containing lines of various lengths. "Subjects" were asked to select lines that were of equal length. Actually, only one person per group was the subject; the others were accomplices of the experimenter. These phony subjects had been instructed to give wrong answers. When the subjects were not pressured by the group, they made correct assessments 99 percent of the time. However, when they made their decisions as part of the group, their correct choices fell to about 60 percent. When they were interviewed after the experiment, some subjects reported that they had gone along with the majority even though they knew that the majority was wrong. Others reported that the group persuaded them that they were wrong. Asch concluded: ". . . the tendency to conformity in our society is so strong that reasonably intelligent and well-meaning young people are willing to call white black."[5]

Even more striking and alarming than Asch's experiment was the well-publicized research of Stanley Milgram on obedience to authority.[6] In Milgram's experiment, the subject or "teacher" was placed in charge of a panel of thirty electric switches which were marked in 15-volt increments up to 450 volts. Above the switches were labels that described the severity of the shock each switch would cause. The labels ranged from slight to severe. The final switch was labeled "XXX" and marked in red. The "teacher" was told to read a series of questions to another subject, the "learner," who was seated at a table with electrodes attached to his body. If the responses of the learner were incorrect, the teacher was instructed to administer an electric shock. Unknown to the teacher, the learner was a confederate of the experimenter, and the electrodes were, in fact, not attached. However, when the teacher administered the shock, the learner would cry out in pain, scream, claim that he had a serious heart condition and could not stand the pain anymore, and, finally, fall silent as though he had succumbed to a heart attack.

Milgram wanted to see just how far the teacher would go. If the teacher refused to administer the shock, a white-coated lab assistant would tell him to continue. If the teacher balked, the lab assistant would assure the teacher, "I will assume responsibility." During some trials, the learner was in a separate room but was clearly visible to the teacher through a glass partition. During other trials, the teacher and learner were in the same room. With the learner in a separate room, about two thirds of the teachers administered shocks all the way up to the maximum. When teacher and learner were in the same room, 40 percent administered a full set of shocks. Even when the teacher had to place the hand of the learner on the shock plate, 30 percent continued all the way to the "XXX" level. Milgram's conclusion: our society has failed to instill in us internal controls on actions that have their basis in authority. In Mil-gram's words:

> The results, as seen and felt in the laboratory, are to this author disturbing. They raise the possibility that human nature, or—more specifically—the kind of character produced in American democratic society, cannot be counted on to insulate its citizens from brutality and inhumane treatment at the direction of malevolent authority. A substantial portion of people do what they are told to do, irrespective of the content of the act and without limitations of conscience, so long as they perceive that the command comes from a legitimate authority.[7]

If normal young adults will misinterpret sensory data when six to eight of their peers disagree with them and similar persons will risk electrocuting others right before their eyes because an authority figure tells them to, should we be surprised at the unprecedented behavior which extremist groups elicit? The Asch and Milgram experiments were carried on in calm, orderly, familiar environments. But what if such staples of the mind-bending, conversion-inducing milieu as sensory overload, guilt induction, disparagement of the individual and his past, disruption of ordinary sleep and dietary patterns, lack of privacy, etc., are added? When a carefully staged and orchestrated atmosphere of hysteria, acute anxiety, and catharsis is deliberately imposed upon a compliant, unassertive, and conformist psyche, conversion will ensue with a high degree of regularity. Whether it will last, whether it will prove integrative or disintegrative of the convert's personality, whether it will produce weal or woe for the convert and his family, cannot be determined at the outset. At this point, I would emphasize one observation: the power of groups is a two-edged sword. Groups provide security and identity while redefining reality and lulling us into conformity. As a group member, the individual will tolerate, permit, and perform acts which he would find impermissible apart from the group. By assuming responsibility for controlling our data input (telling us what is so and what it means) and patterning our moral responses, groups can regenerate us or lead us deeper into our own insanities. They are enormously powerful in these respects. Their mind-bending capabilities are awesome, compelling, and often over-powering. Yet they have no power but that which we confer upon them.

THE ROLE OF THE LEADER

Many of the personal calamities with which I deal arise from the predisposition of the recruit and the particular manipulative techniques of the group. However, there is one additional factor which contributes to much of the harm experienced by individuals in authoritarian groups: the function of the leader. We have mentioned the primacy of one-man (or one-woman) rule in cult and sect groups. We have mentioned the "charisma" of such persons. I find it ironic that a society based on implacable hatred of despotism and unbounded commitment to democratic principles of government would harbor thousands of petty dictatorships which demand the allegiances of hundreds of thousands of citizens. I would state both as an article of my personal faith and as an empirical observation based upon five years of counseling that the child of a free society cannot prosper for long in an anti-democratic setting. Our democratic and individualistic traditions are too pervasive to be easily abandoned. For the expectation of personal happiness and self-fulfillment can be submerged in group goals but it is seldom extinguished. Fortunately, most of my American clients find their capacity for self-abnegation severely limited.

Few cult groups in our history have retained their monarchical form beyond the death of their founder. But even during the lifetime of the founder-prophet, the cult group is no more stable than the individual who leads it. The rule of one over many destroys ruler and subjects alike. Dictatorial power is seductive. It is easily achieved but seldom enjoyed. For not only does absolute power corrupt absolutely, it consumes. No single mind is capable of adjusting the tensions and supplying the needs of ten persons, let alone tens of thousands. And adoration is an addictive drug. There is no such thing as enough unconditional love. The more the leader demands, the more the faithful comply. The more they offer, the more he demands. The more he tinkers with the rewards and punishments through which he maintains control, the more obdurately does reality refuse to adjust itself to his whim. The greater his frustration grows, the greater his hatred of the worshipping throng increases. For his mounting frustration can have, in his megalomaniacal scheme of things, no other explanation than his followers' indolence, faithlessness, and utter lack of dedication. The meekest, most obedient, most self-sacrificing members receive the brunt of the leader's rage. Often they are excommunicated, ostracized, and threatened. Many leave on their own—full of disillusionment and despair —frequently leaving spouses, children, and possessions behind. As a counselor, I do what I can to repair the wreckage. Placing one's fate in the hands of a group is dangerous enough, but entrusting one's destiny to a self-appointed messiah, guru, apostle, prophet, or god is riskier than smoking in a vat of nitroglycerin.

To repeat our earlier contentions: Individuals can get hurt in groups. Some individuals are more prone to getting hurt than others. Some groups go too far. Something should be done about it.

6

"Save the Life of My Child"

FAITH HEALS . . . AND KILLS

Faith heals. Or so contend believers in spiritual healing and deliverance. Faith also maims, blinds, and kills—according to recent reports of court cases and legislative matters concerning cult and sect groups.

On July 2, 1983, Faith Aliano, age ten, died in Woodbury, New Jersey, of complications from untreated juvenile diabetes. Her parents, members of "an unorganized religious sect," hid the body and held daily worship services, praying for her resurrection. On September 12, the body, now partially decomposed, with skin as tough as leather, was discovered by the police. A local Superior Court judge gave the parents three days to arrange for the burial of the child. If they refuse, he said, "I'll consider the county's application" and appoint an administrator authorized to bury the child.[1] Three days later, the couple appeared in court and informed the judge that they refused to comply with his wishes. Mr. Aliano explained: "God said she will come back and that is what I believe." He added: "When the people see her come back to life, I trust they'll begin to believe in God again, because as sure as we're sitting in this courthouse, God is going to raise her." The parents were given six days to comply with the order.[2]

At the same time, in Knoxville, Tennessee, a state appeals court delayed its decision on whether twelve-year-old Pamela Hamilton should be forced to undergo medical treatment for Ewing's sarcoma. Physicians testified that the girl will die within nine months unless she receives immediate chemotherapy and radiation treatments. Her father, Larry Hamilton, pastor of the thirty-eight-member Church of God of the Union Assembly in La Follette, Tennessee, said that he would go all the way to the Supreme Court to keep his daughter from receiving medical care. Pamela and her parents believe that only God can cure her and that it would be an act of rebellion against him to use medicine for the purpose of healing.

According to an Associated Press news story:

> Wearing a blue gingham dress and walking with crutches, the girl gave her testimony Saturday from a couch in the judge's chambers, answering lawyers' questions in a soft, breaking voice.
>
> "I believe that I can be healed without taking treatments and all that," she said. "I don't care what the doctors say."
>
> Asked by a state lawyer if she was ready to die, she replied, "When the Lord gets ready for me."[3]

CHILD ABUSE IN SECTS

In December 1982, an Oklahoma jury acquitted the parents of a nine-year-old boy of charges of manslaughter arising from the child's death from a ruptured appendix. The parents, members of a sect known as the Church of the First Born, were indicted for refusing to allow medical treatment for their son. The parents argued that their religion prevented them from seeking medical help. The jury's verdict was based on the judge's ruling that Oklahoma's laws concerning religious exemptions to child abuse laws could also apply to the couple. Public outcry over the verdict led the Oklahoma legislature to revise these regulations. Under a new state law, enacted in April 1983, the belief in and practice of spiritual/faith healing may no longer be used as a defense in cases of alleged child abuse. According to Charles Green of the Philadelphia *Inquirer*, the legislature decided that "religious exemptions would not apply in cases in which the lack of medical care could result in permanent physical damage to a child."[4] As the author of the statute, State Senator Tim Leonard, explained, "My argument was the child's constitutional rights to life override the parents' constitutional rights to freedom of religion."[5]

A similar case in Colorado had a starkly different outcome. The founders of a sect called Jesus Through Jon and Judy were sentenced to three years' probation for allowing their child to die of pneumonia. The judge overturned the religious exemption because it applied only to recognized religions. The case is being appealed.[6] I wonder if the judge realized that he was involving the state in determining what is and what is not acceptable religion, a task which is clearly forbidden by the U.S. Constitution's declaration: "Congress shall make no law concerning the establishment of religion." Surely the Colorado legislature cannot limit religious freedoms to a list of established, mainline faiths.

On September 29, 1982, a provincial judge in New Carlisle, Quebec, sentenced Roch Theriault (also known as Moses), the leader of a "doomsday religious cult," to two years in prison in connection with the beating death of a child and the castration of a cult member. Theriault had pleaded guilty to a charge of criminal negligence in the death of two-year-old Samuel Giguere, the son of members of the cult, and to a charge of causing bodily harm stemming from the castration of cultist Guy Veer. Veer, who actually did the beating, was found not guilty by reason of insanity and placed under psychiatric care.[7]

On August 2, 1983, Stuart Green, twenty-eight, and his wife, Leslie, twenty-five, were sentenced to one year in jail and fined a thousand dollars upon their conviction of involuntary manslaughter in the fatal spanking of their two-year-old son. The child, Joseph Green, died of shock October 5, 1982, after his parents had spanked him for two hours with a wooden paddle for refusing to apologize for striking another child. The incident occurred at Stonegate, "a self-styled Christian commune" located at Kabletown in Jefferson County, West Virginia.

According to a Washington *Post* article, the child was taken into the farmhouse. Other children and adults formed a circle, while his mother held him and his father spanked his buttocks with a foot-long, half-inch-thick wooden paddle. The beating continued until the child turned pale. His father took him to a local hospital, where he was pronounced dead.[8]

Judge Frank DePond said it was "incredible" that he could not impose a stiffer penalty. The sentencing was interrupted by a man who said that the Greens should be tried for murder. He later apologized.

In imposing the maximum sentence, Judge DePond told Stuart Green: "It is clear that this court had no control over the indictment for the crime you were charged with, but this court finds it incredible that the calculated, deliberate spanking of a two-year-old child over a two-hour period would result in an indictment for involuntary manslaughter, a misdemeanor."

The judge added: "By entering a plea of guilty you have admitted that you killed another human being, a defenseless two-year-old boy, your own child. It is a sad day for our society when a court must intervene to protect a child from its own parents," the judge continued. "Joey's fate is out of our hands today, but your fate is not."

Addressing himself to Mrs. Green, the judge declared: "You abandoned [your] duty when you sat within arm's length of your husband and son, holding and caring for someone else's child, while your own child was slowly being beaten to death." He added: "You could have said 'stop,' or 'don't.' Indeed, you had a duty to interfere."[9]

An Associated Press news photo which appeared in newspapers on Sunday, July 10, 1983, shows Michigan state troopers removing a wooden stock which was confiscated from the

House of Judah religious camp in Allegan, Michigan. Sixty-seven children were taken from their parents and placed in state custody, pending an investigation into the alleged beating death of a twelve-year-old child at the camp. In subsequent television interviews, the House of Judah's leader, "Prophet" William A. Lewis, justified the beatings as the "will of God." He explained that the parents had to make a choice of obeying God and beating their wayward child in accordance with the Bible or of not beating him and risking the eternal damnation of the child's soul. He stated that the parents bore no responsibility for the child's death because God had told them to beat the child. Lewis explained: "God killed him because God doesn't like bad children."[10]

On December 2, 1982, Larry and Lucy Lonadier, members of a seven-adult religious commune which was located in their home in Rensselaer, Indiana, pleaded guilty to involuntary manslaughter in the beating death of their three-year-old son, Bradley. The parents were told by a third commune member that beating the boy with a paddle would save the child's soul. Larry's brother, David, testified that Steven Jackson, who is also charged with involuntary manslaughter in the child's death, urged the Lonadiers to beat Bradley. According to David, Jackson would say, "A butt isn't anything compared to a soul. If you didn't discipline your child, he would probably go to hell."[11]

In 1983 a major church-state dispute emerged in several states, including Arkansas and Florida, concerning the right of civil governments to regulate residential child care facilities run by religious organizations. In May 1983, the Arkansas Child Care Facilities Review Board rejected rules allowing spanking in child care facilities. In so doing, they set aside earlier "emergency rules," which allowed spanking under certain circumstances. Some religious groups claimed that they had been "stabbed in the back" by the Review Board's action. The Reverend Glenn Riggs, president of the Arkansas Christian School Association and pastor of the Hot Springs Baptist Temple, said he "was shocked when I learned that the Board reversed its commitment on the emergency promulgated rules." "We believe we are mandated by our faith . . . to spank," he told the Board. "We believe that very firmly, and we will pursue our faith whether the Board likes it or not." He added: "Simply by the act of your vote you can strike out a basic doctrine of our faith."[12]

Elsewhere in Arkansas, Tony Alamo and the members of the Tony and Susan Alamo Christian Foundation kept vigil around the clock in a prayer room inside the Alamos' sprawling mansion. They knelt and prayed before the coffin containing the embalmed remains of Susan Alamo, who died of cancer over a year before. They were patiently awaiting the resurrection of the controversial evangelist.

Last summer, Tony and his followers began actively recruiting unwed mothers in major cities of the North and South. Posters appeared by the thousands appealing to unwed mothers not to murder their unborn children. Instead, they were urged to accept Tony's offer: "We will pay for the delivery of the child and raise the child until he or she is an adult, educate the child, and pay all expenses until fully grown." When I learned of this campaign, I contacted media acquaintances, suggesting that they look into the matter. Like Arkansas Assistant Attorney General Robert Waldrum, I thought that the Alamos' Christian Foundation might be involved in a black-market adoption racket. However, our best intelligence informs us that Tony is raising "volunteer" workers for his many business enterprises. It would appear that the mothers are required to surrender their infants to married couples in the group at least for two years and until they are married to someone "acceptable" to the group, i.e., a dedicated member.

When Arkansas state social services officials obtained a court order to examine the foundation's child care facilities, they discovered a facility but no children. According to Waldrum:

> Tony has said there were at least 70 children. There were none. We found 17 little beds and four cribs and two potty chairs and one commode. The only heat was from a wood-burning 55-gallon drum. We be-

lieve the women were to have their babies in Memphis. Then they would come to Alma to be proselytized and sent to work. The mother gives the child to Tony.[13]

On September 8, 1983, I received a letter from a legislative analyst for the Florida House of Representatives. Shortly the House will be conducting a "sunset review" of statutes relating to the licensing of residential care for dependent children. Current law, which expires in 1984, requires licensing, with no exemptions except for legal guardians or relatives, for all persons or agencies caring for children away from home. During the 1983 session of the legislature, an amendment was offered which would permit an exemption for a church-related agency which met basic health and safety standards. The amendment was attacked by Florida's two largest Protestant denominations, the Southern Baptists and the Methodists, and was defeated. Totally opposed to the licensing requirement are small sectarian groups which run their own facilities. It is their position that they are answerable only to God and not to civil authority. "We recognize no law but God's," they have told the legislature.

The appeal to a higher authority than the state has been made repeatedly by ultrafundamentalist, independent sects in recent years. Numerous statutes which inconvenience the faithful or restrict their freedom to discipline their children or deny them access to medical care or state-mandated education have been challenged. In most instances, the outcome has been identical to the U.S. Supreme Court's decision in the matter of *Reno County, Kansas,* v. *William and Carol Cowell, also known as Heart Ministries.* On October 6, 1980, the Supreme Court left intact a lower court decision barring the Cowells from running the Victory Village Home for Girls. Since 1972 the Cowells had been operating the home and a related religious school. State officials brought the Cowells to court in 1977, asking that they be prohibited from running the home unless they obtained proper state licensing.

On April 9, 1979, the Kansas Supreme Court upheld a trial

court order that, in the absence of any license, the home be shut down. The Kansas Supreme Court ruled:

> The compelling interest of the state . . . is the protection of its children from hunger, cold, cruelty, neglect, degradation, and inhumanity in all its forms. . . . To fulfill this responsibility, the Legislature has elected to impose licensing and inspection requirements. To these requirements, the [Cowells'] free exercise rights must bow; the balance weighs heavily in favor of those unfortunate children whom the state must protect.[14]

In seeking the intervention of the Supreme Court, attorneys for the Cowells argued: "This appeal concerns the right of religious persons to create a totally religious environment for children, secluded from all worldly matters, in which the basic tenets of the Bible are taught and practiced." Kansas Attorney General Robert Stephan deemed the appeal to religious prerogatives as a way to dodge state licensing requirements "patently meritless." He explained: "The freedom of the [Cowells] to believe as they see fit remains inviolate, but their freedom to act in society is not inviolate and is subject to reasonable regulation by a state for the protection of the society which extends the right of religious freedom."

In November 1982, Lester Roloff, the fiery evangelist whose radio preaching supported controversial homes for rebellious children, was killed when his private plane crashed. In 1973, it was alleged that girls at his Rebehak Home were beaten and starved. Roloff conceded that the girls had been paddled and whipped for misbehavior. He maintained that such discipline was meant to save their souls. "There's nothing wrong with handcuffing a girl to keep her from going to hell."[15] When state officials insisted that Roloff obtain licenses for his homes and maintain state standards, he refused, claiming that the licensing requirement was "Communistic" and violated religious freedom. Upon learning that the Supreme Court had ruled against him, Roloff closed the facilities temporarily and reopened them under the aegis of his People's Church. In

1981, a state court ruled that the church could operate the homes without a license.[16]

In another book, *The Gospel Time Bomb* (Buffalo; New York: Prometheus Books, 1984), I describe several ultrafundamentalist sects with which Freedom Counseling Center has been involved. In several instances, extreme child abuse, wife beating, and avoidance of required medical treatment such as inoculations, removal of operable tumors, setting of fractures, chemotherapy, etc., have been reported to me by my clients. The saddest record of any of these groups is that of Faith Assembly or "Glory Barn," which has its headquarters in the Warsaw, Indiana, area. According to several newspaper accounts, at least fifty-two people—most of them infants and children—have died as the result of following the teachings of the group. Faith Assembly, which was founded ten years ago by the Reverend Hobart Freeman (who is today its pastor), has about two thousand members. Members are discouraged from seeking medical attention on the grounds that only God can heal and that using medicine is evidence of lack of faith.

Reporters Jim Quinn and Bill Zlatos of the Fort Wayne *News-Sentinel* have disclosed:

> There have been twice as many medically unattended deaths as previously reported among those adhering to Freeman's teachings.
>
> Only a small fraction of the 52 known victims were old enough to understand the teachings of Faith Assembly.
>
> An even smaller fraction made their own decision to shun medical treatment.
>
> One victim asked for a doctor a few hours before her death, but no doctor arrived because her husband and friends decided prayer was best for the woman. They prayed for her for hours after she had died.
>
> Routine medical procedures could have prevented many of the deaths.
>
> Faith Assembly deaths were found in Indiana, Illinois, Ohio, Kentucky, Michigan and Missouri.

Seven families suffered more than one death. The
families accounted for 18 of the 52 deaths. Two of the
families lost three members each.[17]

Other newspaper accounts report that a twenty-week-old fetus
was buried in a backyard in a shoe box; babies and their mothers were dying in childbirth while registered nurses looked on
and did nothing; children have died of chicken pox complications; one girl was denied treatment for a massive tumor which
destroyed one eye and finally killed her; a forty-year-old dia-
betic stopped taking his insulin shots and died four days
later.[18] In November 1982, Leah Dawn Mudd, age five, was
removed from her home by court order so that doctors could
remove a cancerous tumor as big as a basketball from her
abdomen. Earlier the girl's four-year-old sister had died of a
tumor. In July 1976, Alice Rogers, twenty-three, a pregnant
church member, bled to death after two days of labor. No
doctor was called.

WHAT SHOULD WE DO?

What, if anything, has been done about this apparent epidemic
of child abuse and neglect? There have been a number of
significant developments—some of which have been mentioned in passing. Courts have not been loath to punish offenders. The media have certainly not ignored the issue. Oklahoma has closed the faith-healing loophole in its child abuse
laws, and a Colorado district court judge has held that his
state's exemption clause was unconstitutional. Further, the
Department of Health and Human Services notified states in
January 1983 that it is no longer requiring them to exempt
religious groups from child abuse regulations.

Meanwhile, Region V Resource Center on Children and
Youth Services announced at its Milwaukee headquarters in
May 1983 that it was willing to allocate up to ten thousand
dollars to stop the abuse and neglect of children in the Faith
Assembly Church. According to Adrienne Heuser, director of

Region V: "It's our position that more can be done for the children involved. If more people knew about the situation and how to deal with it, lives might be saved in the future."[19] The funds will be used for a public education campaign intended to provide information to local prosecutors, public health nurses, welfare department officials, legislators, and members of the general public.[20] State officials have promised investigations of child abuse aspects of the matter (infants and children have accounted for twenty-eight of the fifty-two reported deaths) and inquiries as to whether the "unlawful practice of medicine contributed to the deaths."[21] At least one legislator has indicated that he will introduce legislation designed to prevent the deaths of children whose parents belong to Faith Assembly.

On May 25, 1983, the New York Interfaith Coalition of Concern About Cults, meeting at the City University of New York, issued a statement decrying the abuse of women and children "in many destructive cults" and urging law enforcement officials to "do all within their power to ensure that these victims receive the full protection of the law as applied to their health, education and welfare."[22] The Coalition consists of representatives from the Council of Churches of the City of New York; the Greek Orthodox Archdioceses of North and South America; the Jewish Community Relations Council of New York; the New York Board of Rabbis; the Queens Federation of Churches; the Roman Catholic Diocese of New York; and the Roman Catholic Diocese of Brooklyn. Appealing to "recent research," the Coalition claims that growing numbers of children are being separated from their parents and siblings, receive little or no natal or postnatal medical care, do not have their births recorded, receive little or no education, live in crowded and unsanitary conditions, and suffer from inadequate diet, which damages them physically and mentally. Moreover, the Coalition contends, these children are often sexually exploited and harshly disciplined (often to the point of death). The Coalition also recorded a similar litany of alleged indignities suffered by women in destructive cults, including arranged marriages, interference with existing marriages, inadequate prenatal care, poor nutrition, delivery of children under unsanitary conditions, lack of medical attention, and forced separation from their children.[23]

But the Coalition's statement raised questions in many minds, to wit: Are "destructive cults" any more guilty of child abuse/neglect than our society as a whole? Are cults any more restrictive to and abusive of women than America in general? What is the data base for the generalizations made in the statement—scholarly research or anecdotal reports by ex-cult members and deprogrammers? Is it fair to single out "destructive cults" rather than deal with the broader problem of the role of poverty, lack of education, societal stress, instability, decline in respect for authority, distrust of the medical profession, economic dislocations, and unemployment as contributory factors in America's current epidemic of domestic violence and neglect of health care?

An attempt at answering the question of whether the incidence of child abuse/neglect is higher in cult groups than among the general population was undertaken by researchers at Virginia Polytechnic Institute and State University. Since current cult members refused to return questionnaires to the four researchers, the results are based entirely on the responses of seventy-five former cult members. According to these data, the researchers found that the children of cult members "tend to be more physically abused and receive fewer balanced meals than those of parents not in such sects."[24] The researchers also reported a large number of atrocity stories to support the ex-members' claims. Accusations centered on alleged acts of beatings, confinement, physical punishment, enforced fasting and sleep deprivation, denial of medical care, humiliation and other psychological abuse. The report was attacked as one-sided and biased by Professor Jeffrey Hadden, chairman of the Department of Sociology of the University of Virginia. David Bromley, professor of sociology at the University of Hartford, referred to other studies, which have found that children in cults are not psychologically different from children in the rest of society. Spokespersons for the Unification Church unequivocally denied the allegation of mistreatment of children made by the survey's respondents.[25]

The rescinding of the religious exemption by the Department of Health and Human Services has not been without opposition. The exemption was largely the work of lobbyists for Christian Science, a small but wealthy and influential proponent of faith healing. The 1974 Child Abuse Prevention and Treatment Act read: "No parent or guardian who in good faith is providing to a child treatment solely by spiritual means . . . shall for that reason alone be considered to have neglected the child." Forty-seven states have adopted such exemptions.[26] Now that responsibility for such exemptions has been returned to the states, the Christian Scientists may be expected to be busy indeed. A noted child advocate, Richard Krugman, associate professor of pediatrics at the University of Colorado and director of the school's C. Henry Kempe National Center for the Prevention and Treatment of Child Abuse and Neglect, indicates that he does not consider religious-related child abuse a serious problem. In his words, "I'd hate to see a lot of effort going into stamping this out when you compare 50 or 100 cases of this a year with the millions of children who are victims of child abuse."[27] It is hard to know if Dr. Krugman means that there are only 50 to 100 *deaths* a year in religious sects compared to millions of such *deaths* in our society as a whole or if he means that there are 50 to 100 *known instances of child abuse* in sects compared to millions among the general population. About six cult- and sect-related child deaths are reported to me a year and probably hundreds of instances of child abuse. If there are three million adults involved in over twenty-five hundred cults, as Margaret Thaler Singer maintains, it would seem that the incidence of child abuse is low, although specific instances are often brutal, dramatic, and horrifying.

As the former administrative director of Parental Stress Service of San Mateo County, a multifaceted program for the alleviation of child abuse and neglect, I am well aware that the incredibly high incidence of child beating, neglect, abuse, and sexual exploitation is the secret shame of our society. Even without authoritarian communal groups, America is beset with a vicious overabundance of domestic violence, assaults (physical and sexual) upon women, children, and the elderly, and serious neglect of health, nutritional, and educational needs. Or if one wants real horror stories, the observer should spend a few nights at any state mental hospital, home for the retarded, or facility for juvenile offenders.

THE BASIS OF SOCIETY

Have years of exposure to such abuses jaded me with regard to the offenses of cults and sects? By no means. Incidents like those enumerated above should be investigated and, where appropriate, promptly remedied by action on the part of local police, social welfare authorities, and the courts. Failure to permit needed medical attention for an ailing child or to utilize mandated preventive measures such as smallpox vaccination or other inoculations is a public health matter which must be dealt with through the established channels of public policy. A century of jurisprudential experience with the Jehovah's Witnesses on the issue of lifesaving blood transfusions for minors should provide ample precedent for approaching the problem of the ultrafundamentalist rejection of medicine.

On April 18, 1951, the state of Illinois sought temporary custody of six-day-old Cheryl Labrenz, the daughter of Jehovah's Witnesses parents. The infant was the victim of a medical syndrome which was destroying her red blood cells. Medical testimony established that the child would die without blood transfusions. The parents, Darrell and Rhoda Labrenz, spurned the physicians' advice on the grounds that they were more concerned with their daughter's eternal salvation than with her temporal existence. (Since 1944 blood transfusions have been prohibited by the governing body of Jehovah's Witnesses on the grounds that the consumption of blood is prohibited in the Bible. The proof texts for this position are Leviticus 17:10 and Acts 21:25.) The Labrenzes were secure in the position that even if their baby died, she would surely be resurrected by Jehovah.

The court declared Cheryl a ward of the state for the time necessary to administer the lifesaving transfusions. The Labrenz case was the first of many involving Jehovah's Witnesses parents who refused to allow blood transfusions in life-threatening circumstances. In virtually every case, the courts have ruled that the state's right to preserve and maintain life transcends individual claims of religious freedom.[28] As the court ruled in the case of *John F. Kennedy Memorial Hospital* v. *Heston* (1971), "there is no constitutional right to choose to die. . . . The State's interest in sustaining life . . . is hardly different than its interest in the case of suicide.[29]

The community, through its government agencies, social welfare programs, legislatures, and courts, has the power and the obligation to act. The reason for this has very little to do with the nature of the groups in question. For society's first obligation is to protect the lives and liberties of its citizens, particularly of those who cannot protect themselves. All other liberties, including religious freedom and the right of parents to determine the care and education of their own children, flow from this first obligation. The very foundation of this country is the recognition that the right to life transcends all other rights. All other freedoms must be governed by this principle—in this or in any viable social order.

Although the state may not interfere with the religious beliefs and opinions of its citizens, it can punish religious practices which are criminal offenses.[30] And under the law of most states the failure of parents to provide medical care is a public wrong. If the child is injured from such omission, the parents can be convicted of criminal neglect. And if the child should die as the result of such neglect, the parent may be tried for manslaughter.[31] As a Pennsylvania court ruled eighty years ago:

> The common faith of mankind relies not only upon prayer, but upon the use of means which knowledge and experience have shown to be efficient. . . . In

certain diseases the individual affected may be the only one to suffer for the lack of proper attention; but in other cases, of a contagious or infectious nature, they may be such as to endanger the whole community, and here it is the policy of the law to assume control and require the use of the most effective known means to overcome and stamp out disease which otherwise would become epidemic. . . . "For none of us liveth to himself, and no man dieth to himself," and the consequences of leaving disease to run unchecked in the community is so serious that sound policy forbids it.[32]

In more than a dozen cases involving abuses similar to those listed above, we have discovered that remorseless pressure through the media, child protective services, the police, and the courts throws sect groups off balance, produces self-doubt within members and dissension within groups, unites the previously apathetic local populace in applying pressure to the nonconformists, and, in many instances, leads to the dissolution of the group. If a mother in my community announced that tomorrow at noon she planned to immolate herself and her children in a shopping mall, and if the next day she arrived at the scene with canisters of gasoline, the full coercive machinery of the state would be called into service to stop her suicide-homicide. If she justified her intentions on the grounds that God had told her to do it, the response of the community would be no less tolerant. Unless society protects those who are incapable of protecting themselves, it abdicates its reason for existing. When that happens, vigilantism as strident, fanatic, and harmful as that which it opposes is all that is left.

As we have noted, a new kind of civil disobedience is rampant, i.e., the systematic refusal to obey the law based on an appeal to higher authority. Deprogrammers practice this disobedience in order to "rescue" cultists and other nonconformists. And self-appointed interpreters of God's voice wield "the will of God" as a magic shield to defend them from income tax, property tax, zoning ordinances, health and safety regulations, traffic laws, and any other rules which inconvenience them. The religious man who recognizes no authority but God's (as he interprets that authority for himself) is truly an outlaw. He belongs in no society. The vast majority of religious individuals and religious movements, ranging from the most mainline denominations to the most radical innovative sects, recognize that "the powers that be are ordained of God" and that it is the obligation of each believer to "render onto Caesar the things that are Caesar's and unto God the things that are God's."

The outlaws constitute a menace, without a doubt. That menace springs from the combination of loss of impulse control and otherworldly ideology. People beat children because, under stress, they lose control of themselves, and not because the Bible tells them to. The Bible, as always, is cited in justification of the indefensible. What happens all too often is that sect leaders who are themselves uncontrollably abusive institutionalize their own weakness as a norm for behavior vis-à-vis women and children. In groups with such leaders, the beating of the powerless is engaged in, methodically and deliberately, often while all the members of the group stand by as witnesses, offering their acceptance and support. When conscience, responsibility, and compassion are destroyed by the passions of the angry mob, then persons—the members of the crowd as well as their victims—are reduced to something less than human status. When this happens, the acts which we are observing in today's fringe groups and on the part of deprogrammers are to be expected. They are the manifestations of the spirit of the social pariah, the dispossessed, the disinherited—the behavior of those who have no stake in anything, no love of family, friends, reputation, or themselves. Some cults and sects (but not all) are a haven for such people. The worst examples of child or spousal abuse occur in doomsday sects, groups which see themselves as the last generation of mankind. Why should one worry about the law or decency or propriety or well-being if the world is coming to an end—and soon?

DO GROUPS REALLY CARE?

Look again at the list of newspaper reports reprised at the beginning of this chapter. Is it significant that no incident in my 1982–83 files documents similar abuses by the Moonies, the Scientologists, the Divine Light Mission, the Children of God, or the Hare Krishnas? At most, it tells us that ultrafundamentalist groups more readily lose control and lash out at those who cannot protect themselves. However, it would not be difficult to compile an additional list. Clients drawn from scores of groups, including the five just mentioned, have told me of equally horrifying occurrences—many of which I have verified. It also discloses that the more familiar Bible-based groups receive the censure of the agencies of social control, at least in some communities, long before the more exotic groups. For the former groups draw their members not from wandering dropouts or foreign visitors but from working adults with jobs, homes, and social standing, right across the street.

I should note that having to deal with the intentional infliction of suffering upon children and the deaths of medically unattended women and infants in childbirth constitutes the most emotionally upsetting aspect of my work. However, there are two lessons which I have learned from these disgusting realities. The first lesson: no group can replace parents as sources of stable, caring love. The focus of the group is upon its purposes and seldom upon the offspring of its members. Surrendering the responsibility for child rearing to a sect is like turning an invalid over to a local bridge club. No *group* really cares.

The second lesson is a corollary of the first: in comparison to an allegedly ultimate concern, all other concerns appear ignoble, unworthy, and mere distractions. When the group purpose is not focused upon the next generation as their own and the world's hope for the future, children and women (in their maternal role) become radically devalued, useless, and expendable. As mere objects of little utility for the purpose of the group, they become encumbrances which sooner or later are going to be damaged. I have met loving, devoted, and nurturing parents in every manner of cult, sect, commune, self-help therapy group, and political cell. I know exemplary parents who would never knowingly abuse or deprive their children. But cult and sect groups are largely governed by the whims of manipulative and powerful figures to whom all commitments other than to the mandates of the leader are of secondary importance. Friction between the standards of such authoritarian subcultures and the ethical norms of mainstream society are unavoidable.

7

Counteracting Cults and Sects

INTERVENTION AND FALSE ASSUMPTIONS

Most forms of intervention undertaken by families on behalf of a member in a religious sect or cult are based on the following assumptions: (a) the subject is in trouble—has become dysfunctional, irrational, harmful to himself, etc.; (b) the subject's religious conversion is a psychological aberration; (c) the subject's conversion and subsequent experiences are not authentically his but states into which the subject has been manipulated by powerful agents of mind control; (d) it is necessary to argue the subject out of his newfound faith—otherwise he will remain under the cult's mental domination. The only trouble with this analysis is that it is entirely false.

When a family is distressed by an individual member's conversion, this distress is a *family* dysfunction, often a manifestation of longtime disturbances. Further, conversion is not aberrational. In itself, conversion is neither good nor bad. It is commonplace—an essential element in the religious lives of millions of Americans. The intensity of the experience may throw the individual off balance for a while and the individual may incorporate into his interpretation of his experience elements derived from his group, but the conversion experience itself is the subject's and remains the subject's. A religious conversion is no more a mental disorder than is falling in love or feeling impelled to volunteer to work in a political campaign or having a sudden urge to paint a picture.

Group persuasion is powerful. Individuals in religious groups may surrender to the group an enormous amount of decision making and reality defining. But groups are not all-powerful in their manipulation; nor are individuals capable of handing over total control of themselves. There is an automaticity to human consciousness which absorbs, compares, judges, and discriminates even when we consciously order it not to. How else are we to account for the 75 to 90 percent turnover rate of recruits experienced by even the most sophisticated and manipulative sects and cults?

THE NATURE OF RELIGIOUS EXPERIENCE

In order to develop a clearer conception of the conversion process and the limits of group control, we must have a precise understanding of the nature of religious experience. Religion is a complete restructuring of all elements of a person's experience. An individual's religion is his relationship with that which he regards as central to the nature of things, that which, despite all efforts, he can neither doubt nor elude. And this relationship shapes his thoughts, his feelings, his actions, and the society in which he lives. Religion is an individual's response to that which he experiences as ultimate, as most valuable, as dearest to that person, as most real and intense. Religion is a dynamic living with the gap between the way things ought to be and the way they are. Religion is the impossible dream, the very quest for which gives meaning and dignity to a person's life—even though it can never be attained.

The religion of the convert is rooted in intense personal experience. Most intensity simply evaporates in the light of the next day's sun. Unless a given religious experience becomes the basis of new feelings, attitudes, and behavior, it too will melt away. Most recruits walk away from the Moonies, the Krishnas, ultrafundamentalist sects, guru groups, mass therapies, etc., after a few days. If cults had the irresistible technologies of mind control with which deprogrammers and the Anticult Network credit them, there would scarcely be a soul not in a cult today.

Religious experience is also the whole life of the religiously motivated individual. The sect or cult member who lives in a community of like-minded and like-converted brothers and sisters whose entire lives are devoted to recapturing the ecstasy of the original religious experience in every experience of every kind—the total life of such a person and such a community is a constant religious experience.

Religious experience begins with intensity. It proceeds to symbolism—the need to articulate, explain, and express by attaching vague feeling states to concrete images, pictures, doctrines, rules, and patterns of living. Starting with the emotionally powerful conversion experience, the individual frames all other experiences by reference to it in a process which is both hierarchical and asymptotic. In other words, faith is both the unconditional commitment and the interpretation or frame of reference for valuing all experiences. It is the total act which unites every element in a centered self. Its central element, that in which we believe, is not chosen. It overwhelms us and we see all other aspects of our lives in a new and valued perspective.[1]

Having been overwhelmed by the central element, it is then the vocation of a religious person to "compose" intellectually and existentially a world view which satisfies his rationality by its completeness (inclusion of all experience), consistency, and simplicity, and which remains, at the same time, intensely satisfying.

Even the most zealously defended world view does, at least in principle, count evidence as telling against it. Even though it is accepted unconditionally, it is nonetheless subject to possible revision and even falsification. To accept unconditionally means only the opposite of to accept conditionally—that is, as a hypothesis based upon probability. Experience, whether one wants it to be or not, is an ever-widening, often dialectic (e.g., the inevitable tension between sophistication and simplicity) asymptotic movement to which a structure of reality constantly reacts. From this process not even a world view initially accepted without reservation is exempt. Thus, faith grows, faith matures, sometimes faith dies—even within the most restrictive, authoritarian setting.

When a person commits himself or herself to a way of life, to a way of seeing the world, that person does so with ultimate seriousness. Now, of course, it is the case with an act of personal faith as with any interpretive scheme—even a law of physical science—that the data which are subsequently gathered do not always fit the scheme comfortably. So one has to reinterpret the scheme as incomplete or abandon it altogether. A believer may constantly remodify his beliefs and so gain even higher levels of theological sophistication. However, if through constant modification his faith becomes an embarrassing patchwork of unresolved inconsistencies, then the human tendency to demand simplicity will require that the convert tailor a new garment.

Though there is value in simplicity, there are limits in it as well. Because reality itself is rich and varied, a system of truth must mirror that variety and richness. In other words, a world view must attain a high degree of sophistication. It must be able to allow ambiguities, paradox, awe, and mystery. However, completeness, consistency, and simplicity are not enough. There must be something about a world view which we can feel in our innards. Even when the convert clings to his faith as inviolate and permanent, he cannot escape automatic processes which adjust personal reality to the way things are. No matter how tenaciously the cult or sect disparages the mind, there are rules at work to which a world view is subject. To phrase these rules in the form of questions: Does our way of describing reality suppress, violate, invent, or deceive? Is it complete? Consistent? Simple? Does it satisfy?

CONVERTS AND DEFECTORS

Even without the deconversion efforts of deprogrammers and exit counselors, the fact remains that every convert is a potential counter-convert. The new believer finds that he is anchored by circumstances and responsibilities to a mundane world which stubbornly refuses to disappear. Soon the rapture is gone. The easy answers answer nothing. The new platitudes become old, hackneyed clichés. One's existence again becomes dreary, difficult, and joyless. The magnificent illusion disappears.

The contradictions, inconsistencies, and doubts present within every act of faith cannot be repressed without paying a horrible price—the suppression of critical inquiry, the loveless fanaticism which will tolerate any act of evil. When the inadequacy of one's faith comes crashing down upon the believer, he must grow—even if it means losing his newfound faith.

Why does an individual lose faith? Why is he or she no longer able to interpret the world through a previously meaningful frame of reference? As we have noted, no world view can be strictly proved or refuted. Nevertheless it is constantly subjected to reality testing. Commitment to a community of faith initially releases enormous energy, and the routinization of religious experience is characterized by passion and activity galore. Yet the fact remains that the active phase which follows religious conversion is creatively sterile. Eric Hoffer noted that the strength of the "true believer" derives from his "conviction that life and the universe conform to a simple formula— his formula. He is thus without the fruitful intervals of groping, when the mind is as it were in solution—ready for all manner of new reactions, new combinations and new beginnings."[2] Without such intervals of creative groping, the expressions of the life of faith are likely to be no more than repetitions of the forms already used within the community of faith. Only such intervals can enable the individual or the community to attain new levels of fulfillment. But these intervals are dangerous to the faith which prompted them in the first place, and there can be no guarantee that the faith will survive them. If the community stifles creativity, it will lose its most valuable members. If it grants opportunities for introspection, it may lose them anyway.

TOO MUCH OF A GOOD THING

The primary sources of dissatisfaction with one's faith are (a) *delayed fulfillment,* (b) *hypocrisy,* and (c) *too much of a good thing.* As we noted earlier, religion consists of both the manifestation and the betrayal of ideals which arise from the individual's encounter with the real. Since such ideals are impossible by definition, their actualization may never be more than approximated. Religion is based on the awareness of a gap between what *is* and what *ought to be.* Moreover, it is a program for overcoming the gap—gradually, progressively, and asymptotically. The impossible vision is always the elusive dream. Otherwise it would not be worthy of man's unconditional devotion. But not everyone is cut out for the endless quest. And many sects and cults make the mistake of promising utopia next year or after another thousand souls are saved. When the kingdom recedes into the distant future, many are discouraged and leave.

However, the real tragedy of human religion is not the failure to realize hopeless goals, but the perversion of these goals. The quest for the divine will becomes the quest for power and prestige. The religious group becomes an end in itself instead of a means to the end of human perfection and service to others. This usurpation of the place of God by religion is the greatest source of unsettling ferment within religious communities. The dissatisfaction with the world and oneself which led the convert to the community of the faithful cannot endure hypocrisy. Its existence can be denied only for so long. Finally, inconsistencies between what the group espouses and what it really does deprive the recruit of his motivation to sacrifice himself for the sake of the group.

FUNCTIONS OF RELIGION;
DYSFUNCTIONS OF RELIGION

Dissatisfaction with the group's progress in attaining its goals
and unwillingness to countenance hypocrisy are not the only
ambiguities which undermine the convert's faith. Much more
fundamental are the obstacles arising from the "too much of a
good thing" syndrome. Every valuable function performed by
religion gives birth to a parallel dysfunction. Religion enables
individuals to face powerlessness, frustration, and deprivation.
Sociologist Thomas F. O'Dea describes six functions by which
religion gives security and assurance to human beings to sus-
tain their morale:

1. religion by its invocation of a beyond which is
   concerned with human destiny and welfare, and to
   which men may respond and relate themselves, provides *support, consolation,* and *reconciliation.*

2. religion offers a *transcendental relationship*
   through cult and ceremonies of worship, and thereby
   provides the emotional ground for a new *security* and
   firmer *identity* amid the uncertainties and impossibili-
   ties of the human condition and the flux and change
   of history.

3. religion *sacralizes the norms and values* of established society, maintaining the dominance of group
   goals over individual impulses. It thereby reinforces
   the legitimation of the division of functions, facilities,
   and rewards characteristic of a given society . . .
   thereby aiding order and stability; and . . . the reconciliation of the disaffected.

4. religion . . . may also provide standards of
   value in terms of which institutionalized norms may
   be critically examined and found seriously wanting.

5. religion performs important *identity* functions.
   . . . individuals, by their acceptance of the values
   involved in religion and the beliefs about human nature and destiny associated with them, develop im-

portant aspects of their own self-understanding and
self-definition.

   6. religion is related to the growth and maturation
of the individual and his passage through the various
stages distinguished by his society.[3]

But as O'Dea notes, these very functions give rise to corre-
sponding dysfunctions. By providing emotional support and
consolation, religion may provide an island of security in an
essentially insecure world. Such consolation may encourage a
neglect of this-worldly obligations and an insensitivity to the
responsibilities of everyday existence. It may provide a sense
of identity based upon authoritarian principles which produces a rigid and intolerant personality. Religion may sanction
the status quo, thereby discouraging needed social changes, or
it may so overstate its criticism of present society that it produces nothing but despair. Religion may "institutionalize and
routinize immaturity by providing the individual with *answers*
when he needs to grapple with fundamental *issues* for himself."
The strong sense of identity which it produces may be totally
inappropriate to the individual's life situation.

The functions and the dysfunctions of religion stand in constant dialectical tension. Only the most insensitive fanatic is
immune to this stress. For the most part, religious sects either
adjust to the world in which they find themselves or they
disappear. Likewise, the individual consciousness constantly
remodifies its stances, commitments, values, attitudes, and
feelings or it wastes away. Atrophy is not unknown but it is
rare. Sects and cults during the period of their inception see
themselves as the sole source of truth and goodness. They set
themselves apart from the world, which they regard as beyond
redemption. But if the group survives its first generation, it
comes to terms with the world and takes its place among the
established sects and denominations. It has a stake in being
accepted and respected. Likewise, only the most alienated,
spiteful, and masochistic individuals can maintain a stance of
unreasoning zeal. Cultists grow and mature in, through, and
despite the best efforts of their family members and friends to

deconvert them; in, through, and despite the best efforts of their fellow cultists to protect them from reality; in, through, and despite the cultist's own resolve to sacrifice the qualities which make him human. The processes we have described are automaticities. They simply work whether we will them to work or will them not to.

In other words, most excessive zeal moderates itself. Those who love and are concerned about a fanatic convert should adopt an attitude of patience and hopeful expectancy. The numbers are on their side. Most conversions to cults and sects simply do not last. The most effective strategy is not to debate with the subject as to the merits of the group but to remain scrupulously neutral about the cult while expressing support, confidence, and interest toward the cultist.

A SYSTEM OF RUMORS

Trying to counteract a cult with arguments is like trying to dispel a rumor. In order for a rumor to spread, there must be certain necessary conditions: ambiguity, interest, and arousal. First, there must be a lack of consensus, a distrust of the usual sources of information. Second, the rumor must, in some way or to some degree, personally make a difference to the hearer. Third, there must be present in the hearer an emotional arousal, a state of anxiety due to specific circumstances or habitual personality factors. The individual must be excited about an impending change or disappointed by recent events or confused by occurrences which refuse to conform to the usual categories by which experience is interpreted and absorbed. Or the hearer must be the sort of perpetually overwrought individual who is always searching for a scapegoat to blame for his sense of pervasive distress.

Rumors entertain, explain, justify, express basic emotions, and provide alternative sources of information. A rumor is a factually unverified story based upon conjecture, speculation, wishful thinking, or malice.[4]

Social scientists Ralph L. Rosnow and Gary Alan Fine report that "most rumors are born, have a period of prominence, and then disappear." Rumors are eventually disproved, grow boring and irrelevant, or exhaust themselves through overexposure. But not every rumor elicits responses. Rumors are often met with apathy or active resistance. As economic psychologist, George Katona, observes:

> Mass behavior consisting of cumulative and self-justifying expectations may be viewed as a form of catastrophic behavior. The masses resist speculative fever or despondency unless their sanity is crushed by a series of repeated shocks. The basis of mass sanity may be found in the desire to understand the reasons for developments that take place. News and rumors which are not clearly understood may be accepted for a short while, but they will not sustain action by very many people over long periods.[5]

But what if sanity has already been crushed by inexplicable, unprecedented, and shocking events? What if the individual no longer feels at home in his accustomed world? What if he can no longer accept the justifications, clichés, and explanations offered by traditional sources of authority? When the foundations of his existence are shaken in this manner, his very notions of right and wrong, true and false, acceptable and unacceptable, are placed on hold. And at such times, rumors and systems of rumors provide the only perch on which the individual and group psyches can rest.

In many ways, cults and sects are unified systems of rumor. They are alternative explanations of the way things are and ought to be which have not been confirmed and which probably cannot be confirmed. Whether they are true or false assertions subject to empirical proof or disproof or poetry which cannot strictly be verified or falsified, they give the appearance of being explanations which, at least potentially, satisfy the individual's need for rationality. In addition, they are programs for actions which invite commitment and promise release of pent-up emotional energy. Once such belief systems are planted in the soil of a disoriented, concerned, anxious, and excited psyche, they are governed by the same dynamics as the successfully disseminated rumor. They are just as difficult to uproot but they may definitely be counteracted.

Percy H. Tannenbaum has noted that attitudes are changed as the result of cognitive incongruity.[6] Consider the hypothetical example of one respected authority making a negative statement about another accepted authority. Imagine that the U.S. Public Health Service issued a statement that regular brushing of the teeth destroys beneficial enzymes and is harmful to the health of the whole body. The conflict between the two accepted authorities, the U.S. government and the dental profession, could cause a shift in attitude which, in turn, could produce a change in behavior (lack of dental hygiene). Now, such being the case, Tannenbaum asks, how can this negative shift in attitude be eliminated or reduced? Extensive experimentation by Tannenbaum found that there are four effective procedures, which appear to have a cumulative ameliorative effect when used in combination: (1) denial of the assertion; (2) derogation of the source; (3) logical refutation of the assertion; and (4) strengthening the original concept through counter-argumentation.

The same four steps are the basis of conversion, deprogramming, and exit counseling. The standard technique for recruiting consists of attracting the individual's attention by focusing upon his disorientation, concern, anxiety, or excitement; gaining his confidence through shows of affection and approval; setting up the system of his accustomed beliefs in straw-man fashion by belaboring the negative aspects of the individual's present life and the shortcomings of the society in which he lives; denigrating parents, college, friends, the media, et al. as the source of this distressing way of life; presenting a new system as an escape from the psychic pain of the old; representing the founder-prophet of the group as a trustworthy and enviable source in contrast to the prior sources; enjoining attitudinal and behavioral compliance with the new system; and rewarding the desired response with peer approval and affection. There is no special magic or "technology of mind control" at work here. Rumors are spread and discredited in the same way.

The deprogrammer creates a situation to which the subject cannot but respond with attention, excitement, anxiety, and confusion. Life in a cult or sect is an endless process of intellectual accommodation, interpersonal relating, personal striving, assimilating of novel experiences, reevaluation and reinterpretation of ideology, and spiritual transformation. The deprogrammer reduces the complex social/theological/psychological life of the cult or sect to a list of assertions and then proceeds to deny these assertions; to ridicule their source; to refute them through arguments, evidence, and the testimony of previous defectors; and to strengthen the original world view (values, attitudes, associations, affective ties, family relationships, friendships, career orientation, etc.) which the convert spurned when he joined the cult or sect. Since deprogrammers are usually more successful at tearing down new commitments than at shoring up previous attitudes and patterns of behavior, their deconverted subjects are frequently left in a state of ambivalence, depression, undirected anger, and unrest. Such "floating" is blamed upon the damage to the central nervous system allegedly wrought by cult brainwashing. Discredit a rumor being spread by a highly anxious individual—one who considers the rumor a valuable possession, an expression of his being and worth—and similar affective states will manifest themselves.

What the agent of deconversion is really witnessing in the former cult recruit are mourning phenomena. Whenever an individual is suddenly separated from someone or something which he fervently loves, from someone or something which defined his personhood, he suffers "floating" symptoms. If I were to learn that I were the victim of a terminal illness, I would, according to Elizabeth Kübler-Ross, pass through the stages of denial and isolation, anger, bargaining, depression, and, finally, acceptance. All profound shocks to our sense of identity and security elicit similar responses. When a marriage ends, the psychological aftermath incorporates anger, rage, sadness, depression, a deep sense of guilt and personal failure, shame, regret, fear and distrust of the formerly beloved, nostalgia, the desire for reconciliation, a confused sense of identity or ego boundaries, self-justification, and, ultimately, acceptance and coping. Why should separation from the friends, accustomed routines, beliefs, mores, pains and pleasures of an all-consuming lifestyle be any less traumatic?

Cult recruiter and deprogrammer alike reduce reality to the level of rumor and gossip so that they may destroy the subject's presuppositions and implant their own. When examined dispassionately, we discover that the assertions, denials, arguments, and evidence of both are cognitively unimpressive—almost trivial. For instance, the high divorce rate does not prove that most people are unhappy and that they should become Moonies and allow Sun Myung Moon to select ideal mates for them. A high divorce rate may equally be cited as evidence that many people were once unhappy, did something about it, and are now much happier. Further, even if divorce is caused by unhappiness, there is no empirical evidence that Moon-arranged matches are any more fulfilling or that they are longer-lasting. The logic of the cult recruiter and the deprogrammer alike is based upon the "fallacy of the missing middle." In terms of conventional philosophical logic, to jump from the assertion "Socrates is a man" to the conclusion "Socrates is mortal" requires the "middle" premise "All men are mortal." The logic employed by recruiters and deconverters attacks given assumptions—e.g., the potential convert is loved by his parents; the potential deprogrammee can find personal fulfillment by returning to his career goals; the cult leader is set apart from and superior to ordinary human beings; or the cult has failed to achieve its goal of establishing an egalitarian society. By demolishing such premises the recruiter/derecruiter acts as though he has destroyed the entire system of thought, belief, attitudes, and behavior from which the premises have been plucked. However, from a logical point of view, it should be recognized that the refutation of any premise does not require the abandonment of a lifestyle, nor does it necessitate the acceptance of an alternative.

DISCREDITED BELIEFS

Gossip is highly susceptible to counter-gossip. Gossip loses much of its power when it is denied, the motives of the gossipy individual are maligned, arguments or sophistries are presented against the gossip, and the trustworthiness of the target is reasserted. However, it is imperative that the counterattack upon lies or speculations should never repeat the rumors which the counterattack seeks to still. The technique employed by many corporations of taking out full-page advertisements which print both the rumor and the denial are heavy-handed and counterproductive. When these denials are paraphrased in newspaper, magazine, radio, and television accounts, they give far greater prominence to the rumor than to the rebuttal. Further, they provide an authoritative source which may be cited (out of context, to be sure) when the rumor is next repeated: "The New York *Times* says that Procter and Gamble is owned by the Moonies (or by Satanists). *The Wall Street Journal* says that McDonald's hamburgers contain earthworms (or Jack-in-the-Box uses horsemeat). Dan Rather says that several children have been killed when their stomachs exploded after they swallowed Pop Rocks, a sizzling candy, together with Coca-Cola." It would be much more effective, in my opinion, if Procter and Gamble planted stories about who really owns them—their stockholders. Rumors may be alluded to ("Certain rumors have been spread by irresponsible individuals . . ."), but they should never be reiterated. But even more effectual is the spreading of a new, more interesting, more colorful, more disgraceful, more bizarre story about some other subject.

Much cult recruiting and much deprogramming repeat the mistake of spreading a rumor through its denial. The cult indoctrinator urges that the convert break off all contact with the "evil" world outside the cult—family, friends, associates, and the media. So, of course, many cult members sneak into public libraries, bootleg letters to friends, and contact "negative" persons or "persecutors" of the group like me. Likewise, the deprogrammers' insistence that the defector end all ties with friends in the group and zealously avoid thinking about cult life, ritual, prayer, chanting, etc., when combined with the self-fulfilling prophecy of "floating," contributes to a great deal of nostalgia for the group and to an obsessive ongoing identification with the group. Many ex-cultists adopt roles as anticultists with a zeal and one-sidedness which is just as fanatic as their former role within the group. They need a new rumor—a new story about themselves meaningfully related to the world in which they find themselves and about the world in which they find themselves as meaningfully related to them. In sum, they need a sense of direction, identity, and hope for the future. They do not need substitute dependencies. They need freedom.

8

Is Force Ever Justified?

THE "BRAINWASHED" STAR

About two years ago, a young man convinced me, without a shadow of a doubt, that his wife, who had left him to live with another man, had been radically depersonalized through beatings, sexual humiliations, theft of her earnings, involvement in criminal activities, etc., and further that she was in danger of committing suicide. Since the sincerity and honesty of the husband—confirmed by polygraph examination and extensive corroborating testimony—were being beyond question in my mind, I offered to do whatever I could to help.

I naïvely hoped that I could help mediate their differences. But when we attempted to meet with her, the young woman refused to talk to either her husband or me. She told several people in our presence that my client was not her husband but a crazy person who had forged her name to a marriage license. Her husband next sought the advice of local attorneys and an experienced woman psychiatrist. Believing that his wife's life hung in the balance, he petitioned the court for a temporary commitment so that she could be examined at a mental hospital. And I testified in support of his petition. The order was granted, but the examining psychiatrist released her after a brief conversation and nothing more could be done. The young woman had her marriage to my client annulled on the grounds that she was previously married to someone else but had not known it at the time she married my client!

I probably had no business getting involved in this case in the first place. I am a counselor of individuals and families disrupted by cults, sects, and other authoritarian groups. But like all who have established a reputation for helping those perplexed by cultism, by 1982 I had become a "court of last resort" whenever anything "cultlike" or suggestive of "brain-washing" or "mind control" was considered part of one party's problem with the life and behavior of another party. I set out in 1979 to establish myself as a professional who takes seriously the problems of families caused by the conversion of a loved one to a nontraditional religious group, and who offers noncoercive and informed alternatives to forcible deconversion techniques. But no matter how many times I protested being introduced as a deprogrammer at my Rotary Club, no matter how frequently I begged the media not to identify me as a deprogrammer, no matter how deliberately I dissociated myself from deprogramming when potential clients sought me out, it was never enough. Since a significant part of my work—and a highly successful part in my clients' hearts and minds—is the persuading of zealots to cool their ardor and return to reason and moderation, I am lumped together with the agents of coercive deconversion by virtually everyone familiar with my work—except by the real agents of coercive deconversion! Certainly no deprogrammer considers me a yoke-fellow.

And because my work has been perceived by the media as somehow "anticult" it is assumed that I belong to the general field of anticult agitators. After all, I am forever issuing warnings about obnoxious groups and doleful tendencies. And, further, since most anticult rhetoric concerns "brainwashing," "mind control," "snapping," "floating," "coercive persua-sion," and the like, I have come to be seen as an expert on this agenda of terms despite my disavowal of the concepts and the activities which the uncritical use of these terms provokes and justifies.

Moreover, because I have received public notice for having aided many of the Jonestown survivors and for exit and reentry counseling of Moonies, Hare Krishnas, et al., I must surely be an expert on "brainwashing." But that perception of my expertise overlooks one vital consideration: I do not believe that the Templars or the Moonies or the Hare Krishnas or 99 percent of converts to the myriad other cults are brainwashed at all. For, in my opinion, "brainwashing" should be restricted to instances of acute depersonalization accomplished through the use of force and life-threatening stress. Unless the subject believes that his situation is hopeless, that escape or rescue is unlikely, that cooperation with one's captors and tormentors is the only way to survive, and that suicide is the only viable alternative, we are not dealing with true brainwashing at all but rather with the much more familiar and obvious processes of persuasion and conversion.

I am an expert on such areas as religious experience, fundamentalism, sectarianism, contemporary religious movements, and new age communities, and on the problems which result from conversion phenomena and deconversion phenomena. Since scores of my subjects have been referred to me with problems resulting from their having been forcibly deconverted by techniques more compatible with the characteristics of brainwashing mentioned above, I am in a way an expert on acute depersonalization. But only on the attempted depersonalizing and repersonalizing of religious converts. Beyond that I am wandering in terra incognita.

So when the distraught husband, mentioned above, was referred to me by a principal arm of the Anticult Network and when he told me about the decade of alleged sadistic cruelty which his wife had suffered, and when his stories were confirmed by many of his wife's friends in response to my telephone inquiries, I came to a conclusion which I had never before (or never since) formed with respect to anyone, subject or not. I concluded that she had been radically depersonalized or "brainwashed." Do I still believe that the lady is "brainwashed"? Not really. I believe what many persons have told me. She is a highly impressionable person who is comfortable with life in her chosen field and competent in dealing with little else. Her personal life is governed by a recurring pattern of submission to a strong male, being betrayed by her beloved, fleeing from her lover, resenting and vilifying her love, becoming despondent, seeking a new knight on horseback, repeating the process with him, and then, inevitably, returning to her original love-hate relationship. I feel sorry for her and I pity anyone who attempts to rescue her in the future.

What is significant is that I would be recommended for this case by a prominent anticult agency and that an expert on cults would be an appropriate source of help in such a matter. What it tells us is the extent to which forms of intervention which arose in response to cults and sects have increasingly been applied to matters unrelated to cult conversion.

FORCIBLE CONFINEMENT

There is a legitimate place for forcible confinement. That is why our society builds prisons and mental hospitals. And criminal deeds and acts which demonstrate that an individual is dangerous to himself/herself or others are good reasons for confining a person. But these should be the only reasons. Thoughts, convictions, beliefs, or attitudes should never be the basis for denying a person's freedom of action. But if a person's actions would be considered crimes or evidence of insanity—whether or not he or she belonged to a socially deviant group—then the use of confinement through the machinery of the criminal justice system or the mental health commitment laws is totally justifiable. If a person breaks the law, he should suffer the consequences whether he believes that he is God, an apostle, a prophet, or a carpet beetle. And if a person is murderous or suicidal, society has an obligation to protect itself from that individual and that individual from himself—even if that person believes that God is ordering his destructive acts. Further if a person is so disoriented that he or she is unable to care for the basic needs for food, shelter, and clothing, then it is the obligation of one's community, through its social services and mental health services, to see to it that those needs are met.

In addition to my knowledge of religious cults, I am an expert on the slowness of the courts and the unresponsiveness of police and social service agencies. In both the state of Delaware and the county of San Mateo, California, I was the initiator of "patient advocate" projects to help the mentally ill cut through red tape in order to obtain the services and protections guaranteed them under the law. Through my personal efforts, the infamous Biggs Building at Delaware State Hospital was closed and the inhumane conditions at the same institution's Springer Building were rectified. Obtaining adequate professional help—even where there is money for it—often proves arduous. I also know that mental health commitment statutes in many states have been redrawn to protect the civil rights of potential patients. I was the co-author of the "enlightened" commitment statutes in the state of Delaware. Before this revision, it was possible to commit a person to the State Hospital virtually on a whim. After the enactment of the 1973 statute, it became virtually impossible to commit anyone— even a person desperately in need of treatment. A compromise statute was enacted. But despite the imperfections of the system and the laziness, indifference, and incompetence of all too many social service and criminal justice officials, we are a society of laws. And an act of lawlessness, no matter how well intentioned, is essentially an antisocial act.

THE "DEATH WISH" SYNDROME

Deprogrammers maintain that their activities are indispensable if our society is to be preserved. They see themselves as vigilante forces of law and order protecting us from alien subversion, the destruction of the family, and disregard for our laws and traditions. I am sure that the character portrayed by Charles Bronson in the movie *Death Wish* would sympathize with their attitude. After all, his "surviving spouse/father of helpless victims takes law into his own hands and exterminates the baddies" epic espouses the same philosophy. But I find that there is something terribly perverse about this vigilante logic. And I cannot accept it.

Watching a loved one go down the drain is a dreadful and frustrating experience. Seeing potential wasted, idealism prostituted, and thought replaced with the rote recital of vapid platitudes is a gut-wrenching, sleep-stealing, heartbreaking nightmare. One of my clients is a writer whose attractive, intelligent, and loving daughter walked away from her last semester at college to become the custodian and sole support of a highly disordered elderly man who believes that he is a shaman. Living on a starvation level, working menial jobs, ignoring her health needs, the young woman has deteriorated by the month. During some visits by her parents, she was warm and open. At other times, she was hostile and accusatory. She notified local authorities that her parents intended to kidnap her. As their concern for their daughter's health and sanity grew, the parents sought help from every conceivable source —police, mental health professionals, the Anticult Network, and myself. I could help them improve their communication skills, encourage them to be aware of the underlying family dynamics which were being acted out in their confrontations with their daughter, explain the origin of the spiritual/philosophical mélange being spouted by their daughter, but I could do nothing more. The situation worsened appreciably. The financial plight of the cult of two left them living on the streets of skid row. My client could take no more. Without informing me, he contracted for the services of a deprogramming team. The snatch was poorly planned: the father and his agents were apprehended almost immediately. The father was arrested, arraigned, indicted, and stood trial on charges of kidnapping. For a long time, the local district attorney intended to make an example of him and was pressing for a felony conviction. Finally, undeniable evidence of the physical and mental health needs of the young woman and her guru moved the prosecutor to allow the father to enter a plea of guilty to a minor offense—assault. The young woman and her guru now live in the back of a pick up truck.

Young adults constantly make decisions which we, their parents, see as mistakes. And how many of those forewarned and anticipated disasters ever really happen? And how many of them are as irrevocable as we fear? Potentially calamitous, illegal, and costly interventions should be a rare and final resort. Instead, such acts are increasing in number and spreading into areas far afield of cultism. The reasons for the spread of coercive intervention are to be found in the following brief history of the anticult movement and deprogramming.

THE ANTICULT NETWORK

The Anticult Network (ACN) is a loose-knit confederation of parents' groups, deprogrammers, and cult-concerned mental health professionals. The major elements of the ACN are the following:

1. Citizens' Freedom Foundation—a poorly organized, erratically funded, and essentially volunteer-staffed association of more than fifty small activist groups concerned with the problem of "destructive cultism." Both the Canadian group, COMA (Council on Mind Abuse), and the Boston-based American Family Foundation, John G. Clark's base of operations, are "associate" members of the CFF family. I would estimate that the total number of individuals involved in CFF activities throughout the country is less than one thousand. Most of these are parents of young adult sons and daughters who were formerly involved in cult groups, particularly the Unification Church, the Divine Light Mission, the Church of Scientology, the Way International, and various smaller Bible-based sects and "guru" groups. Although the CFF national organization is officially opposed to kidnapping, two thirds of those actively involved in CFF are vehemently in favor of coercive deprogramming, and most of them have used the services of such big-name deprogrammers as Ted Patrick, Joe Alexan-

der, Sr. and Jr., and Galen Kelly. CFF boasts a parallel organization, FOCUS (Former Cultists Support Network), a council of former cult members, most of whom have been successfully deprogrammed from such groups as those mentioned above.

CFF is basically an educational organization, an information and referral service, and a lobbying organization. Most CFF chapters consist of a few pairs of parents of former and present cult members. Their efforts tend to be extremely disorganized, lacking in coherence, and unprofessional. During one recent twelve-month period, the organization went through three executive directors. Also there is a high level of paranoia, which is partially justified by past efforts at infiltration by agents of the Church of Scientology. Many CFF chapter leaders are so afraid of cult reprisals that their phone numbers are not listed. This makes it very difficult for new supporters to join CFF or even to find CFF. A convention of CFF chapters and their supporters from among the deprogrammers and cult-concerned mental health professionals is held annually. The 1982 conference in Washington, D.C., drew more than eight hundred participants.

2. Deprogrammers. Allied to CFF in the anticult crusade are approximately forty individuals who work full-time or part-time as active agents of deconversion. Popularly known as *deprogrammers,* this group is available for hire by concerned parents for fees averaging twelve thousand dollars per case. The activities of deprogrammers typically consist of abducting cult converts, forcing them to reconsider their allegiances, creating a stress-overload situation which is eventually resolved in successful cases by the subject's renunciation of the group. Two deprogrammers are former truck drivers; one is a private detective; many are ex-cultists who themselves were deprogrammed; several are born-again Christian zealots who regard cults the work of the devil. There is a category of noncoercive or "voluntary" deprogrammers who usually refer to themselves as "exit counselors"—a term introduced by the author. "Exit counselors" include some mental health professionals, a large number of former coercive deprogrammers whose wings have been clipped by civil and criminal court

cases, former cult members who are opposed to force, evangelists for various evangelical Christian groups, clergymen of
various faiths, etc. However, it should be noted that noncoer-
cion is the exception rather than the rule among the practition-
ers of the ACN.

3. Cult-concerned mental health professionals. There is a
small company of anticult "shrinks." These psychiatrists, psychologists, and social workers are extremely important to ACN
because they provide a professional legitimation for
deprogramming, for the advocacy of anticult legislation, and
for anticult propaganda. The chief role of these professionals
within the ACN is to describe as psychologically destructive
the conversion to lifestyles which parents find socially unacceptable. Accusations of brainwashing, mind control, and hypnosis thus become the basis for extralegal and religiously sup-
pressive ACN activities.

The ACN began about ten years ago with the efforts of
parents opposed to their offspring's involvement with the
Children of God, a fundamentalist group of the most obnoxious type. COG having been driven out of the United States
within a short time as the result of Ted Patrick kidnappings and
anti-COG publicity, a new target or targets were required. As
with any newly emerging institution, the deprogrammers and
the anticult parent groups had too much invested in the ACN
to simply fade away. The Hare Krishnas, the Moonies, and the
Divine Light Mission soon became the foci of anticult efforts.
These efforts won very little public support and had practically
run out of steam by late 1978. Public, media, and legislative
bewilderment at the mass murder and suicide of more than
nine hundred U.S. citizens at the People's Temple enclave in
Guyana in South America revivified the spirit of the ACN. For
about two years the chief targets remained the Moonies, the
Hare Krishnas, and DLM. By last year the Unification Church
had passed its zenith and was having serious recruitment difficulties in the United States and England; the Hare Krishnas
were no longer visible on the streets of major urban areas, and
they had experienced severe organizational upsets after the
death of their founder; and DLM had shrunk to a tiny minority

position within America's nontraditional religious movements. Efforts were made to direct major attacks upon the
Church of Scientology, but this group proved a ruthless, cun-
ning, and dangerous opponent.

BORN-AGAIN ANTICULTISTS

Another source of anticult propaganda is to be found within
the fundamentalist or evangelical Christian camp. Three major voices of Christian anticult fervor are the Spiritual Coun-
terfeits Project, Berkeley, California; Christian Research Institute, Anaheim, California; and InterVarsity Christian
Fellowship. I would point out that the born-again Christian has
other criteria for applying the pejorative term "cult" to specific groups than do the supporters of the ACN. It is not the
brainwashing and the psychologically destructive nature of a
group which necessarily lead to that group's condemnation as
a cult by the born-againers. Rather the fundamentalist attack is
based upon theological considerations. Since the groups
which the born-againers attack are "selling" something other
than the necessity to repent of one's sins and accept Jesus as
one's personal saviour, these groups are regarded as dangerous, satanically inspired spiritual deviants. The born-againers
condemn est, Life Spring, Transcendental Meditation together with the ACN enemy list (the Moonies, the Hare
Krishnas, Scientology, DLM, COG, etc., etc.) and, in addition,
such classically non-evangelical groups as the Mormons, the
Jehovah's Witnesses, Christian Science, and Bahai. The sin of
these groups is that they do not proclaim the born-again Christian version of personal salvation. The SCP list of "counter-
feits" grows and grows. The CRI issues warning after warning.
Fundamentalist anticult groups have condemned rock music,
women's lib, Dungeons and Dragons, the wearing of native
American jewelry, the importation of clothing and artifacts
from the Orient, and the teaching of the theory of evolution.
While such hostile cult-baiting is not typical of evangelical

Christianity as a whole, there is a xenophobia at work in the born-again movement which is lamentable. For instance, Cullen Davis, a wealthy evangelical businessman, destroyed more than a million dollars' worth of gold, silver, jade, and ivory art objects because evangelist James Robison told Davis that they were graven images of the heathen. However, it is one thing for me to refuse to respect these groups intellectually; it is quite another for me to ignore their influence. That I clearly will not do. Since more than forty million Americans consider themselves evangelical Christians, what a handful of anticult opinion makers among them say must be of grave concern. And these opinion makers are daily adding new groups to the list of non-Christian cults, saying that the newcomers are as much cults as the Moonies, the Hare Krishnas, Scientology, and the People's Temple. The evangelical attack upon these groups adds a great deal of credibility to the ACN assault. And many of the most active ACNers and deprogrammers are themselves born-again Christians. Once a group is demonized by the ACN as a "brainwashing cult" and by the SCP et al. as a "spiritual counterfeit," it becomes fair game for the entire spectrum of anticult assaults—propaganda, litigation, and forcible deconversion.

9

Targets of
the Anticult Network

The beginning of the ACN may be dated from the emergence of two interrelated events in San Diego about ten years ago. Ted Patrick deprogrammed his first COGer. And a grass-roots organization emerged in reaction to the Children of God. The group bore the name FREECOG, meaning "free our children from the Children of God." Parents of concerned COGers met, commiserated with one another, exchanged intelligence about COG activities, and attempted to develop strategies for limiting the growth of the sect and for getting their sons and daughters to leave the group. At about the same time, a parents' auxiliary group named THANKCOG had formed to counteract the horror stories which were being spread in an effort to discredit COG and to express parental appreciation of the role that COG had played in rescuing their sons and daughters from street lives of crime and drug dependence.

THE FREECOG–THANKCOG DEBATE

We should not forget the background of the FREECOG–THANKCOG debate. The cults of a decade ago were "counter-countercultural" phenomena. First came the great exodus of middle-class Americans to the suburbs after World War II and an attendant escalation in the standard of living as measured by the acquiring of goods (homes, vacation homes, appliances, second and third automobiles, etc.) as well as the ability to purchase services which were seen as adding to the quality of life (orthodontia, golf and tennis instruction, adult education, Montessori nursery schools, hairstyling, horseback riding lessons, etc.). The dark side of affluence was the ever-increasing need for the purchase of services which served to readjust adults to their lifestyle when the stresses of that lifestyle threatened to overwhelm them. (Remember that much of the affluence of the last three decades was based upon sending mothers into the labor market and thus destabilizing the status quo of Mom in the kitchen waiting for Johnny and Mary to come home from school so that she could take Johnny to Little League and Mary shopping for her prom dress. Divorce, alcoholism, deaths from stress-related diseases, and psychiatric and psychosomatic disorders ceased to shock us but became familiar if disquieting occurrences. And among our adolescent children drug use, delinquency, promiscuity, vandalism, accidental deaths, and suicides became endemic and epidemic. Mothers were going to work and fathers were taking second jobs so that their families could have what they had never had as children—including the disappearance of the family itself. In my mind, the symbol of these years was a friend of mine who popped Dexamil, a prescription drug which combined dexedrine [a stimulant which suppresses appetite] and Miltown [a tranquilizer] so that she could lose weight and remain sexually attractive while coping with the stresses of being the divorced working mother of two frenetic daughters and the lover of an underemployed architect.)

UNTIDY REVOLUTIONS

We were in the midst of a number of overlapping and untidy revolutions. There was "black power," the strident and some-times violent reminder that our society has yet to reconcile the pretensions of equality with the realities of racism. There was the "sexual revolution," inspired by *Playboy* magazine and ren-dered convenient if not instantly conventional by "the pill." There was "women's liberation," the total reexamination of traditional male/female roles. There was the introduction of the word "ecology" and a growing awareness that the industri-alization which underwrote our prosperity was inconsistent with a sense of stewardship with respect to our nation's and our planet's resources. There were "peace marches," antiwar riots, and draft protests directed against American involve-ment in the Vietnam War. And there was ecumenism and the Second Vatican Council, the former to foist big-business con-cepts of strength through merger upon Protestantism, and the latter to open the windows of the Roman Catholic Church to the fresh air of secularity. There was the "third force" in psy-chology, the death-of-God theologians, the pop art and the op art painters, and, above all, the call to "turn on, tune in, and drop out."

I have before me a fourteen-year-old copy of Rasa Gus-taitis's *Turning On* (New York: Signet, 1970). This account, to quote the front-cover copy, of "one woman's journey to the outer limits of America's new psychic frontiers" already looks like a relic in my library with its $1.25 price (for 288 pages) and the yellow dye of the page edges mingling with the oxidation which will turn the paper into ash before my remaining brown hair turns white. It is the frontispiece offering "Other SIGNET Titles of Special Interest" which catches my eye. For there offered at prices ranging from seventy-five cents to $1.50 (plus ten cents to cover mailing costs) are the following:

> *The Marijuana Papers* edited by David Solomon. In this basic reference work on marijuana, the author calls on works from Rabelais to Terry Southern, Baude-laire to Allen Ginsberg, as well as evidence from lead-

ing pharmacologists and sociologists, to show exactly
what effects the controversial drug has and to expose
as illogical the fears which Americans have reacted to
its use *[sic]*.

Confrontation on Campus: The Columbia Pattern by Jo-
anne Grant. A revealing, day-by-day account of the
Columbia University rebellion which serves as a pro-
totype for student revolts across the country.

The Hippie Papers by Jerry Hopkins. An eye-opening
collection of outspoken articles from the nation's un-
derground press on subjects ranging from LSD to
free love, from Vietnam to police brutality.

My Self and I by Constance Newland. The intimate,
completely frank record of a woman's experiment
with LSD, the controversial "mind-expanding" drug.

Where It's At by Garson Kanin. It's the uptight, now
scene of parent and child, unable to agree on a common sense of values and bridge the generation gap.

I have quoted this page in its entirety, with only publisher's
identifying numbers and prices removed, to enable the reader
to share my rediscovery of this time capsule from not so very
long ago. For it provides the context for understanding the
emergence of (a) those religious sects now known as cults
(both biblical—like COG, the Tony and Susan Alamo Christian Foundation, and the Way International—and Oriental—
the Divine Light Mission, the Hare Krishnas, and Transcendental Meditation); and (b) the ACN and deprogramming.

Many of the street people and hippies of the sixties became
the COGers, Jesus freaks, Krishnas, meditators, premies
(DLMers), etc., of the early seventies. For they had discovered
that a life based solely on rebellion against middle-class mores
—an "alternate lifestyle" which is characterized by endless
self-gratification, principally by means of tripping, screwing,
uttering obscenities, protesting, and attending rock concerts,
or talking about tripping, screwing, uttering obscenities, protesting, and attending rock concerts—becomes a boring, sti-
fling, depressing dead end.

Not every dropout became a cult recruit. Some died. Some got menial jobs. Some became professionals. A few went to Vietnam. Others ended up in mental hospitals. Many are now living on agrarian communes. Some tried wandering incessantly from therapy group to Zen monasteries to yoga villages to Indian ashrams. But many thousands needed a firmer sense of identity and direction, a feeling of belonging to someone or something, some limits and rules. Without being able to articulate the process, they were drawn to any leader or any movement which promised the ecstasy and heightened intensity of their vagrant ways without the grave risks of death, insanity, meaninglessness, and despair. The children were looking for pied pipers. Pinocchio no longer wanted to go to school, but he did not want to turn into a donkey either.

Ten years ago, when I interviewed the adults who are today known as cult leaders, I found that the major operative word in their vocabularies was the same word favored by today's deprogrammers—namely, "rescue." These leaders were saving the wretched refuse of the counterculture from annihilation—from addiction, dope dealing, prostitution, starvation, homelessness, and disease. How could such unloved and unwanted discards be rescued without the imposition of strict discipline? Very few of the converts of the early seventies whom I met were experiencing any hassle from home—for often there was no home. No one cared. And lest we lose perspective, we should note that the same is true today. The parents of the vast majority of cult recruits are involved in no form of anticult activity and want no form of intervention.

In the early seventies it was much more socially acceptable to praise the new sects as valuable experiments in personal rehabilitation and social reform than to criticize their superficiality or to question their totalitarian tendencies. And how dangerous a threat could they possibly be? Consider the original targets of the ACN—COG, the Unification Church, the Divine Light Mission, and the Hare Krishnas. There have never been more than ten thousand American COGers, five thousand Moonies, twenty thousand DLM premies, five thousand initiated devotees of Krishna Consciousness. If we were to throw in the forty thousand dedicated Scientologists and the twenty thousand followers of the Way International, what are we talking about? A hundred thousand cultists. A third of 1 percent of our population. Do cultists constitute a significant force when contrasted with America's estimated forty-four million evangelicals, who comprise one fifth of our population?[1]

However, because the anguish of those parents whose children are among the tiny sample mentioned above cannot simply be ignored, I have never forgotten that when a fanatic cult holds the allegiance of one's son or daughter, it holds 100 percent of that child's heart and mind—even if the group to which the individual belongs represents a millionth of a percent of the population. Ted Patrick's perception of COGers as "mindless robots" who had been deprived of their free wills through "on-the-spot hypnosis" and "powerful techniques of mind control" made someone other than COG recruits and their parents responsible for the zealotry, antimaterialism, irrationality, paranoia, and disdain for their parents which the COGers expressed. When differences of opinion and lifestyle set parent and adult offspring against one another, there is usually nothing which the parents can do but shake their heads and complain to one another. But when deprogrammers claimed that the recruits had been brainwashed, and when powerful negative metaphors were added to the explanation— the Manson family murder of 1969, Patty Hearst's apparent conversion to the SLA in 1974, and finally the mass murder/ suicide of nearly a thousand men, women, and children at Jonestown in 1978—then parents have not only a point of view which makes them totally right and their children completely wrong but an ideology which explains why their children are wrong, excuses their children of culpability, and offers a form of intervention to restore their children to their right minds.

Patrick and his ilk rescued a small percentage of COGers. Media coverage of the activities of the deprogrammers and FREECOG blackened COG's reputation, as did a deprecating report on COG by the New York State Charity Frauds Bureau. At the same time, David Berg's theology and ethics skidded toward the sewer. In 1973 Berg announced that his teaching had supplanted the Bible as the ultimate source of truth. In 1974 Berg ordered fornication for the purpose of recruiting. Advocacy of lesbianism, incest, and the sexual exploitation of children would follow. The kidnappings multiplied, each new case providing COG with persecution, which is the surest way of confirming the rightness of fanaticism in the fanatic's mind. When every effort to maintain enthusiasm proves futile and a religious movement is losing steam, persecution never fails. So Moses David (Berg) warned the faithful that cataclysms would soon ravage America, said farewell to the United States, and took most of his constituents with him to greener pastures— the Canary Islands, Libya, England, Italy, Switzerland, and Central America. And everywhere the prophet went, deprogramming was sure to follow.

THE MOONIES AND THE KRISHNAS

The emigration of COG spread the ACN and deprogramming to England, Spain, and beyond. But since few American parents can afford to send deprogramming teams abroad and few non-Americans can pay to import them, the ACN/deprogramming business would have gone bankrupt if it had not been for other "cult" groups which took center stage as COG withdrew from the spotlight. From the mid-seventies on, one group has been the "cult" by which all other manifestations of "cultiness" are measured: the Moonies—the Unification Church of Sun Myung Moon.

In the period 1975 to 1981, the Unification Church was recruiting about fifteen hundred young adults a year at the New Education Development/Creative Community Project in northern California. Its rate of turnover was ferocious—about 90 percent of its converts would leave, most of them within the first six months. But the deceptiveness of Moonie recruitment —the recruiters' failure to disclose ties with the Unification Church until the potential convert had been softened up by peer pressure, conviviality, affection, and intense indoctrination—and the deliberate interference with the convert's maintaining of family ties brought strong parental reactions. This gave the now entrenched de-culting apparatus a new supply of clients. Parents of Moonies—both deprogrammed and obdurate—turned to the ACN. Deprogrammed Moonies, generally more articulate and disciplined than ex-COGers, swelled the ranks of deprogrammers.

The isolation of those Hare Krishnas who dropped out of their worldly involvements, their preoccupation with neo-Hindu philosophy, their obsessive chanting, their obtrusive fund raising (in airports), and their bizarre appearance made curiosities of them. (They are the cult most frequently depicted in motion pictures, usually comedies.) They became the easiest targets of deprogrammers—easy to find and easy to abduct.

But the Moonies and the Krishnas had the money, organization, and toughness to counterattack. Soon deprogrammers and parents were being sued by unsuccessfully deprogrammed young adults, arrests were being demanded by civil libertarians, and procult activists, such as the Alliance for the Preservation of Religious Liberties (APRL), and mainline denominations and evangelicals were expressing their disapproval of the ACN's interference with the free expression of religious choice.

THE PUBLIC BECOMES BORED

But by 1978 the general public had become bored with the whole spectacle. There are only so many ways to tell the deprogrammers' story. The story of each new deprogrammee added nothing to the tale of last year's apostates. One despondent parent sounded like another. Deprogrammers amassed a "book" on each cult like a catcher's "book" on each batter in his league. This material quickly found its way into the press. Such data were usually restricted to two or three major disconfirmations or inconsistencies. For example, the Unification

Church cannot be of God because it uses deception. The Reverend Moon owns a factory which manufactures machine-gun parts. Four Moonies committed suicide in an eighteen-month period. The Way International distributes anti-Semitic literature and promotes marksmanship at its college. Guru Maharaj Ji watches cartoons on television and has thrown a follower into his swimming pool.

Before long every nasty detail had been revealed. But who cared?

THEN JONESTOWN

Public interest faded. Until Jonestown.

The wires of media attention crackled: *A "cult" killed nine hundred people. There are thousands of cults—millions of cultists. Each cult is a potential People's Temple. All cultists are brainwashed. All cult leaders are insane, greedy, oversexed, murderous, hypnotic—just like Jim Jones.* The post-Jonestown mentality applied the terms "cult" and "brainwashing" to every sect, meditation group, missionary movement, commune, mass therapy group, and association of like-minded friends. "Destructive cultism" became a matter of legislative concern. Senator Robert Dole convened an investigating committee with no official legislative status just to demonstrate that "the government was concerned." Two fundamentalist sects were placed in receivership by the California attorney general. State legislators considered conservatorships which would allow parents of cult converts to remove them for deprogramming. Such a law was passed in New York State by two successive sessions of the legislature, but failed of enactment due to the governor's pocket veto on the first occasion and his direct veto on the second.

Cults became big news. My wife was right. Publishers tripped over one another to tell the Jonestown story. "How I was brainwashed by the Moonies" was the basis of about fourteen books. Similar but less numerous accounts of defections from COG, the Jehovah's Witnesses, DLM, the Old Orthodox

Church, and various assorted groups filled the shelves of bookstores. CBS television presented a two-part docudrama on Jonestown, *The Guyana Tragedy,* and followed with the made-for-TV movie *Blinded by the Light,* which depicts a cult recruit, who is rescued from a vapid brainwashing cult, and his sister, who is dismayed by the need for the deprogramming but eventually supports her family's decision to have her brother kidnapped. Theatrical releases included the superbly produced *Ticket to Heaven* (the true story, with names changed, of the conversion and deprogramming of a Moonie), the amateurish *Moonchild* (the true story of the conversion and deprogramming of a Moonie with Moonies and deprogrammers played by ex-Moonies and deprogrammers), and the stillborn *Split Image* (the purely fictional story of the conversion and deprogramming of a non-Moonie featuring an evil cult leader, an unprincipled deprogrammer, stupid parents, and general nonentities).

Once again, who cared? The books sold poorly. The movies attracted small audiences. Two major conferences scheduled for California university campuses were canceled for lack of registration. The Center for the Study of New Religious Movements in America, a much-heralded project of the Graduate Theological Union (Berkeley), quietly closed its doors in 1983 after four years of operation. Evangelical cult watchers returned to old, familiar enemies like the Mormons, the Jehovah's Witnesses, and the Christian Scientists. Two books on cults were withdrawn from circulation when costly litigation resulted. Yet cults remain of great interest—to those who have children in them, to those who have left them, and to agents of intervention employed by families disturbed by them.

The cult boom was short-lived. All the hoopla and hysteria were directed at a handful of fanatic sects which had passed their zenith and were in decline by the time the first first-person account had appeared. The counterculture is history. The hippies are long gone. The sects which served the needs of the dropout from the world of the dropouts have either declined or developed fresher merchandise. The prospective cultee of the mid-seventies and early eighties is simply not a hippie. The potential convert is more likely to be a college graduate who cannot find a challenging job or a young professional who is having difficulty establishing a clientele or a divorced mother with two children who cannot maintain her family on welfare checks.

Consider my own subjective statistics. In 1979, I spent more time with Moonies than Sun Myung Moon did. In 1980, the Unification Church, the Church of Scientology, and the Way International comprised three quarters of the Freedom Counseling Center caseload. In 1981, there was an upsurge in groups headed by Indian and neo-Hindu gurus and a significant number of cases involving fundamentalist Christian aberrations—i.e., Bible-based sects with leaders who claim to be God's only prophet, an apostle, or Jesus Christ returned. By 1982, errant evangelicals of a charismatic, deliverance, and survivalist bent occupied 70 percent of my attention, followed by the "cult of the nineteen-year-old boyfriend"* and other family disputes which were initially misperceived as cult-related problems. The number of first-time cases involving the Unification Church, Scientology, DLM, and COG had declined precipitously. In 1983, there was a sudden surge of Hare Krishna cases—voluntary walk-aways reflective of the internal struggles now convulsing the International Society for Krishna Consciousness (ISKCON)—but the operative words have been "Bible" and "brainwashing." In a previous chapter, I

---

* At Freedom Counseling Center, we use this phrase to refer to attempts on the part of distressed parents to redefine problems having nothing to do with cults or mind-bending as cult-caused. A few years ago, a mother phoned me and reported that her daughter had been "brainwashed by a cult." I asked what was the basis of her assumption. She replied that her eighteen-year-old daughter was living with a nineteen-year-old boyfriend. "She must be 'brainwashed,' " the woman insisted. "She's never done anything like this before."

The young woman subsequently returned to college. The parents, still convinced that she was brainwashed, have become actively involved in the Anticult Network.

have described the cults of the eighties and the characteristics of their clientele. And in the next chapter, our attention turns to the manner in which the ACN and the deprogrammers have responded to shifts in their market. For while publishers and producers pulled their hair, the ACN had already retooled. The issue would no longer be "cults" but a state of mind of which cults are but one manifestation.

10

Brainwashing and Deprogramming

DEFINING DESTRUCTIVE CULTISM

In the early seventies, the major ACN issue was cults. What was a cult? According to the ACN literature of that period, a cult was a missionary religious group based on the allegiance to a leader with absolute power. A cult engaged in witnessing, proselytizing, and solicitation of funds. A cult had beliefs and rituals (such as chanting, speaking in tongues, prayer, meditation, etc.). Cults were described further as sexually immoral, life-denying, thought-disparaging, law-breaking, brainwashing, controlling, and violent. Cult converts, it was claimed, were recruited through deception, were hypnotized or brainwashed into becoming glassy-eyed robots or zombies, and underwent incredible personality and behavioral changes. Cult members were said to labor long hours for no wages, to dress in peculiar costumes, to eat unnourishing food, to be deprived of sleep. Anticult psychologists, psychiatrists, and sociologists described cultists as suffering from thought control, coercive persuasion, mindlessness, loss of freedom of choice, thought reform, trancelike states, damaged health, limited self-concepts, impaired logical reasoning, and regression to the level of childlike dependence. Such persons would readily abandon school and family relationships, sell everything and give the money to their cult leaders, and assume a new identity.

In sum, a cult was a high-demands religious sect which brainwashed its members. The three essential elements were "religious," "demanding," and "brainwashing." However, anticultists who were themselves religious—e.g., Catholics, Jews, and born-again Christians—subtly removed the religious dimension by redefining cults as "pseudo-religions." If a cult is not religious at all but only pretends to be, then we are left with "demanding" and "brainwashing" as the necessary and sufficient definers of cultism. So any group which brainwashes the unwary into joining and brainwashes its converts into doing as they are told—that is, acceding to the demands of the group or leader—is a cult.

There were other reasons for removing the characteristic "religious" from the list of obnoxious traits. It is quite possible for a young adult to convert to a movement which, in the eyes of established religious "authorities"—even authorities respected by the convert's parents—is theologically orthodox yet unacceptable on other grounds. Many leading ACNers are Jews who are opposed to missionary movements which encourage young adults to leave Judaism. Yet many of these movements are accepted and supported by large segments of the evangelical Christian community—America's most influential religious population. My own history, which has led from religiously uncommitted Judaism to evangelical Christianity to a middle-of-the-road denominational Protestantism, is just as threatening to such Jewish ACNers as conversion to the Hare Krishnas. In fact, deprogrammings of Jews from evangelical groups such as Jews for Jesus, Crossroads, and Maranatha are commonplace.

Evangelical Christian parents have the same problem when their children join fundamentalist communal groups such as the Northeast Kingdom Church (also known as the "Yellow Deli") in Island Pond, Vermont, or Truth Station in Apple

Valley, California. Billy Graham or Jerry Falwell could scarcely fault their theology, for they subscribe to the articles of faith which set fundamentalists apart from other Christians. However, there are issues of lifestyle, child rearing, and ministry which separate born-again father—e.g., an independent Baptist—from born-again son, a member of the Northeast Kingdom Church. Hence, born-again communal groups are hard hit by deprogrammers and raked over the coals in ACN publications.

Evangelical sociologist Ron Enroth exemplifies the dilemma. In a speaking appearance in Pomona, California, he referred to "aberrational Christian groups," including the Walk, the Way International, the Church of the Living Word, the Bible Speaks, and the Church of Bible Understanding.[1] According to Enroth: "They're right along the edges of evangelicalism and fundamentalism and very difficult to define."[2] So if these groups cannot be defined or readily distinguished from acceptable evangelical sects, how can evangelical parents justify deconverting their children from them? Likewise, in a society which tolerates cross-cultural changes of religious allegiance, how can Jewish parents engage in forcible counter-conversion of converts to Christianity? The solution has been the dropping of religious criteria from the definition of "cult."

In reality, the ACN has become the anti-brainwashing league, an association of parents who have attempted to deal with their children's disavowal of parental attitudes, values, and moderation with immoderate rhetoric and radical intervention. Why? Because a mental dysfunction or a brain disease or a thought disorder placed their children (who average about twenty-three years of age) in grave jeopardy, annulled their civil rights, and necessitated extreme remedial actions.

WHAT IS BRAINWASHING?

The term "brainwashing" came into the language shortly after the Korean War. It had been coined by British journalist Edward Hunter in 1951 and was popularized by Richard Condon's novel *The Manchurian Candidate*. It referred to the techniques through which the North Korean military obtained the cooperation and compliance of captured UN troops, including Americans. Using "thought reform" methods similar to those used in Red China to "reeducate" so-called bourgeois elements after the Communist take-over, the North Koreans were able to persuade American POWs to sign confessions that they had participated in acts of unlawful aggression, including germ warfare, and, in a small number of cases, to renounce their U.S. citizenship and resettle in North Korea or Red China.

The North Koreans, it should be recalled, accomplished their objectives through a combination of physical brutality, psychological pressure, intensive indoctrination, and clever manipulation. And they had almost limitless time in which to apply their techniques. As Alan W. Scheflin and Edward M. Opton, Jr., note in their excellent work *The Mind Manipulators:* "The most central element of brainwashing, as that term has classically been applied to prisoners, is the deliberate breaking down of identity, the reduction of the individual ego to a helpless cipher."[3] According to these authors, the process has three major components: (1) The "stripping away of symbols of individuality." The prisoners are dressed uniformly and drably. Their hair is cut uniformly and drably. They are separated from their "buddies." They are not allowed status based upon military rank. They are denied the use of their own names. (2) The induction of self-betrayal. The prisoner is coerced into committing acts of which he is deeply ashamed, such as betraying comrades, confirming the enemy's intelligence on the disposition of friendly troops, divulging information on the morale of friendly forces, or making statements critical of the command or political leadership of friendly troops. (3) Mobilizing guilt. Through relentless questioning, the captors discover what the captive feels guilty about. The captors harp upon it remorselessly and continually.[4]

As North Korean brainwashing has further been explained by Louis Jolyan West, chairman of the Psychiatry Department at UCLA and director of the UCLA Neuropsychiatric Institute, the main elements of the Communists' method was "DDD"— debility, dependency, and dread. Captives were deprived of their vigor and healthfulness until they grew weak—but never seriously ill. They were required to ask their captors' permission for "every little thing" until they became totally dependent. And they were subjected to never-ending threats of death and torture, which were reinforced by humiliations such as being paraded in chains before hostile crowds of enemy civilians.[5]

Just how effective was brainwashing as a means of compelling ideological conversions? Not very. As the testimony of numerous POWs from the Korean and Vietnam wars reveals, forcible thought reform fails to work on POWs subjected to years of harsh treatment and grueling interrogation. During the Korean conflict, about 3,500 American POWs survived the "death marches." Fewer than fifty collaborated on propaganda statements; fewer than twenty-five refused repatriation; and fewer than ten have failed to return home. As practiced by the North Koreans, brainwashing was not that effectual. Communist propaganda and our own misdirected reactions to Communist propaganda made brainwashing seem much worse than it was. A study of American military history discloses that the behavior of our POWs was really no more shameful than during earlier conflicts and certainly nothing compared with the number of POWs who changed sides during our Civil War and warred against their former friends. As Robert Jay Lifton remarks in *Thought Reform and the Psychology of Totalism* (the work which has become the "deprogrammer's Bible," the source of proof texts to demonstrate to the subject that the cult has "brainwashed" him):

> Behind this web of semantic (and more than semantic) confusion lies an image of "brainwashing" as an all-powerful, irresistible, unfathomable, and magical method of achieving total control over the human mind. It is of course none of these things, and this loose usage makes the word a rallying point for fear,

resentment, urges toward submission, justification
for failure, irresponsible accusations, and for a wide
gamut of emotional extremism.[6]

The myth of brainwashing was a convenient way of assigning
blame to the North Koreans for the failure of our own troops.
It was much less ego-deflating to explain that the Communists
had some secret way of reducing POWs to mindless puppets
than to recognize our own inadequacies in coping with our
own unwillingness to accept the frailties of our own soldiers. I
have never in my life heard the word "brainwashing" used
when it did not connote on the part of the user the attitude: "I
cannot accept and I will not accept what you are doing. And I
will not accept any responsibility for it. Nor will I allow you the
dignity of accepting responsibility for it."

I am in total agreement with the "antipsychiatry psychiatrist" Thomas Szasz, M.D., on this point. As Szasz has written:

> The critical question thus becomes: What is "brain-
> washing"? Are there, as the term implies, two kinds
> of brains: washed and unwashed? How do we know
> which is which?
>
> Actually, it is all quite simple. Like many dramatic
> terms, "brainwashing" is a metaphor. A person can
> no more wash another's brain with coercion or con-
> versation than he can make him bleed with a cutting
> remark.
>
> If there is no such thing as brainwashing, what does
> this metaphor stand for? It stands for one of the most
> universal human experiences and events, namely for
> one person influencing another. However, we do not
> call all types of personal or psychological influences
> "brainwashing." We reserve this term for influences
> of which we disapprove . . .[7]

BRAINWASHING AND THE ANTICULT NETWORK

I wonder how seriously the first applications by the ACN of the concept of brainwashing to religious cultism were? When people are upset with one another's stubbornness, they often accuse each other of being brainwashed—particularly when a third party is seen as an influence. But they rarely mean that the third party has obtained attitudinal conversion through physical brutality, psychological pressure, intensive interrogation, etc., in a totally regimented and controlled environment. Such loose usages have been commonplace for thirty years. And "brainwashing" has been frequently applied both popularly and academically to religious phenomena. The critics of revivalism have often accused Billy Graham, Oral Roberts, tent evangelists, Campus Crusade for Christ, et al. of brainwashing. British psychiatrist William Sargant explored the parallels between mass evangelism and North Korean brainwashing in his 1957 book, *The Battle for the Mind,* and at about the same time, D. A. Windermuller, a Boston University doctoral candidate, compared and contrasted Communist brainwashing techniques with the methods used to induce religious conversion during the eighteenth-century evangelical revivals. The scholarly examinations left me with the impression that there are techniques for making people feel uncomfortable and ways to offer them the adoption of a new identity as a means of escaping that discomfort. The techniques are not all that mysterious—they have been used by salesmen, politicians, prophets, and pimps for centuries. "Brainwashing" is a term of opprobrium, which indicates that the speaker does not approve of the consequences of the process upon the subject. "Conversion" and "reform" are terms which indicate the speaker's approval of the results.

Ted Patrick gained notoriety for seriously applying the term "brainwashing" to religious cults and for the coercive methods which he justified on the basis of such alleged brainwashing. Patrick's world is as dualistically black and white as any cultist's. The universe is divided into heroes and villains. The villains have mysterious "ESP mind control" powers which enable them to hypnotize or brainwash gullible youth on the spot. During the indoctrination phase, the brainwashers implant posthypnotic suggestions which continue to control the recruit for the rest of his or her life. Through deprogramming, the mind is forced to return to life and work once more like a recharged automobile battery. The key element in the reversal of brainwashing is the skillful use of interrogation, asking the cult "victim" questions which he or she cannot answer on the basis of the cult-formatted programming. But the implanted suggestions continue to threaten the deprogrammee, causing him or her to "float" between cult and post-cult identities. The solution is to isolate the deprogrammee from possible cult influences, redirect his or her attention away from possible cues which would retrigger the posthypnotic suggestions (e.g., Patrick discourages deprogrammees from reading the Bible), inundate the subject with affection, attention, and entertainment, and involve him or her in deprogramming activities as soon as possible and for as long as practical. This summary of the Patrick approach is derived from his book *Let Our Children Go,* various interviews which have appeared in the media, and my own conversations with him and members of his organization.

Patrick is a semi-literate, virtually uneducated former truck driver who is totally unfamiliar with scholarly/professional examinations of hypnosis, mental illness, conversion phenomena, family therapy, etc. He is not a theorist but an activist, a self-appointed warrior against dark forces. He believes that American religious cultism is the creation and pawn of Communism, a means of overthrowing America by subverting the minds of the young. He is a conspiracy theorist who believes that virtually all tragedies of the past generation (political assassinations, mass murders, terrorism, and the like) were deliberately caused by "the Communists" and are the direct result of Communist experiments in mind control. Now that his repeated convictions for kidnapping and the huge costs of his defense attorneys' fees have diverted him from active involvement in snatch operations, he is advertising that he has developed a new, improved treatment for brainwashed victims which does not require coercion, takes only forty-five minutes to four hours, can readily be taught to anyone, and will soon be made available in reasonably priced seminars. He described the innovative approach in remarks made before the 1982 national conference of Citizens Freedom Foundation. "It's simple," he explains. "All you have to do is locate the hypnotic suggestion, reach into the mind, and remove it."

Granted that Patrick's intervention was "successful" in hundreds of cases (though it scarcely achieved the more than 90 percent deconversion rate which he claims) and further granted that his former associates, deprogrammees, and imitators have spread the good news that the brainwashed can be forced to think again, Patrick has been a total failure as an ideologist of his own point of view. This task has been left to others—John G. Clark, Jr., M.D., the Boston-based psychiatrist, and writers Flo Conway and Jim Siegelman, in particular.

MASSIVE DISSOCIATION AND MIND CONTROL

It was about eight years ago that John G. Clark, Jr., M.D., entered the lists as a champion of anticultism and an enemy of the "absolute dangers to mental health and personal development" posed by conversion to the "new youth cults."[8] Clark's involvement with anticult efforts apparently began in 1976 when he was called upon by a colleague whose twenty-year-old son, Ed Shapiro, had joined the Hare Krishna movement. When Dr. Shapiro learned that his son intended to give a twenty-thousand-dollar trust fund to the International Society for Krishna Consciousness, the elder Shapiro hired Ted Patrick, who held the Shapiro boy against his will at his parents' home while attempting to "deconvert" him. Patrick's effort being unsuccessful, young Shapiro returned to the Hare Krishnas. Deprogramming having failed, Ed's father asked a nearby psychiatrist, Dr. Clark, for help. Without examining Ed, Clark informed a local court that the young man was "incompetent" as a result of "mind control." On the basis of

Clark's opinion, the court denied the young Shapiro access to his inheritance, giving control of the money to his parents. Ed was ordered to enter a mental hospital, as Dr. Clark later explained, "to have determined whether Edward Shapiro has been subjected to coercive persuasion or mind control, and the extent, if any, to which such mind control prevents or precludes diagnosis of mental illness."

Up to this point, Clark had spoken with Ed for only fifteen minutes. Yet the judge granted Clark's recommendation and Ed was admitted to McLean Psychiatric Hospital, where Clark diagnosed him a "paranoid schizophrenic." However, Clark's colleagues at McLean disagreed with this diagnosis. They found no evidence of any mental disorder, concluding that Ed was neither incompetent nor under "mind control." But Clark continued to contend that Shapiro suffered from a borderline personality, evidence of which was his choice of membership in an absolutist cult. In other words, Ed's joining of the Hare Krishnas was proof that he was mentally ill.

Dr. Clark was later investigated by the Massachusetts Board of Registration and Discipline in Medicine for his role in the Shapiro case. According to the Massachusetts Board: "There is no recognized diagnostic category of mental illness of 'thought reform and mind control.' " It added: "Moreover, the basis on which this 'diagnosis' was made seems inadequate, as mere membership in a religious organization can never, standing alone, be sufficient basis for a diagnosis of mental illness." "There seems no factual basis," the Board concluded, "either for the conclusion that Mr. Shapiro was mentally ill, or that he was a danger to himself. Again, this invites the concern that the judgments were based entirely on the subject's religion."

Subsequent to Clark's involvement in the Shapiro case, he has emerged as a leading anticult expert witness in judicial and legislative affairs. To cite a few examples: In August 1976 Clark testified before the Special Investigations Committee of the Vermont Senate Investigating the Effects of Some Religious Cults on the Health and Welfare of Their Converts, testimony which was introduced into the *Congressional Record* by Leo J. Ryan (November 3, 1977). In many instances Clark has testified in court as to the mental state or competence of individuals whom he has never examined.[9] For example, Clark testified on behalf of a young woman deprogrammed from the Church of Scientology. Although Clark had never examined her prior to his testimony, he found Scientology culpable for being a "dangerous cult" which recruited its members by inducing a "trance state" by means of a "narrowing of consciousness" or a "dissociation." Apparently believing Dr. Clark's account of the alleged psychological devastation inflicted upon the plaintiff by the Church of Scientology, the jury awarded the young woman the sum of two million dollars. (This award was subsequently reversed upon appeal.)

In a recent case, Clark testified that a woman had suffered a manic-depressive episode as a result of having taken one weekend of the est Training. Although he admitted that he had never taken or observed the est Training, he contended that the est trainers employ hypnosis or trance induction in order to elicit delusions of grandeur. Upon cross-examination, he stated that he had never been hypnotized and had never induced a hypnotic state in a patient. Yet solely on the basis of his examination of the defendant, he was able to deduce that she had been hypnotized during the est Training and that the Training had caused her mental disturbance. The court held otherwise.

It is the "induction of dissociative . . . states" which is the key to understanding Clark's theory of the mental health hazards of religious cultism as well as his conclusion that "est precipitated a severe psychotic break, which, without est, may have been avoided completely."

Although Clark never offers a definition of the term "cult," he states that cults' "total U.S. membership extends anywhere from 3 to 10 million people involved in more than 3,000 groups ranging in size from two or three members obeying a guru to many thousands." It would appear, if I understand Clark correctly, that what makes a group a cult is the use of *a technology of mind control*—that is, techniques of thought reform or brainwashing which are, in his words, "very similar overall although each [group] uses its own peculiar style." Clark finds these techniques used by the Hare Krishnas, the Unification Church ("Moonies"), the Church of Scientology, the Divine Light Mission, such political groups as the Weathermen, Communist cells, terrorists, some Hasidic Jewish groups, a large part of the Transcendental Meditation movement, elements of the Episcopal Church, and even the "born-again phenomenon of today." Clark notes that this "brainwashing" has materialized in all of these groups "within a reasonably brief historical period—as though to a signal."

An outline of Clark's general theory is as follows: Involvement in a religious cult and in many other groups, including est, causes a mental illness—that is, "a malfunctioning of the central nervous system causing substantial disability because of alterations of consciousness, mood, memory, perceptions, orientation or capacity to test reality." "The necessary and sufficient contributant to this mental illness is systematic maintenance and pathological consequences of massive dissociation." Ideology is inconsequential. It is the "quality of the experiences" and not their content which is crucial. The induction of a trance state is achieved by isolation and overstimulation. The subject experiences a state of uncritical receptivity which permits him to absorb much information in a short period of time, which renders him suggestible to threats of supernatural punishment, and which leads him to experience unusual or altered states of consciousness such as "mystic-like reveries." The sustaining of the dissociative state by the skillful manipulation of the subject alters the basic controls of the central nervous system. As Clark states repeatedly: "The menstrual periods may stop, or beard growth may be substantially slowed." The prolonged trance state changes personality drastically and dramatically. The original personality undergoes a "mutilation." Continuous dissociation produces personality changes and behavior disorders which, contends Clark, the clinician would associate with chronic temporal lobe epilepsy or chronic schizophrenia. Cult conversion, he adds, resembles temporal lobe epilepsy in the following clinical respects: deepening of all emotions, grandiosity, depression, suicide, irritability, overt hostility, violent crimes, murder, loss of libido with hypersexual episodes, and paranoid suspiciousness.

In some subjects, says Clark, a formal thought disorder develops which is "not immediately distinguishable from that of schizophrenia." Prolonged dissociation may result in permanent changes in brain function. If a subject remains in a cult-induced dissociative state for four to seven years, he becomes totally acculturated and depersonalized. This "shift in personality," cannot be treated without the use of extraordinary measures (coercive deprogramming) which are not legally or ethically available to mental health professionals. What is required, it would appear, is a combination of antipsychotic medication and maintaining physical control "for long enough to bring about the confrontation therapies which might be effective in reestablishing the original personality style in the way it was done with Korean War prisoners." Although it is Clark's opinion that deprogramming has been successful in effecting repersonalization, he notes that former converts who have been deprogrammed may suffer from depression, shame, psychotic episodes, and suicide. In addition, they are susceptible to reconversion and a gradual degradation of ordinary thought processes, decline in IQ, loss of judgment, and loss of ability to form intimate human relationships.

What if we were to ask Dr. Clark to tell us whether all dissociation is harmful? Clearly, this is not his position. For states of dissociation include "moments of falling apart, pieces of the mind changing, the sense of reality changing, these are the moments of great spiritual happenings, sometimes brief hallucinations, craziness, falling in love . . ." Without dissociation there would be no "creative syntheses." It is only *induced* and *maintained* dissociation which is always harmful. What if we should ask Clark: Does all prolonged dissociation lead to thought disorders indistinguishable from schizophrenia; and to permanent, harmful changes in brain functions; irreversible acculturation; depersonalization which psychiatrists are helpless to treat without the use of coercive deprogramming techniques? Clearly, the answer to this question would be in the affirmative. And may it be safely inferred that when such coercive deprogramming is applied in an attempt to remedy the harmful effects of dissociation, at worst the deprogramming can be successful but potentially lead to psychosis or suicide? Or at best, the deprogramming may be successful but potentially lead to the degradation of the reconverted subject? Once again, the answer would have to be yes. Or that the attempted deprogramming could fail and that the effort could leave the subject even further acculturated and depersonalized? Yes, again.

If we understand Clark correctly and have rightly assumed that it is not dissociation but prolonged dissociation which is psychologically destructive, then it would be appropriate to ask further whether or not such prolonged dissociative states are limited to cultic phenomena. And here is the real bone of contention between Clark and myself. It is my contention that prolonged dissociative states are extremely common in our society. They are found everywhere—alcoholism, drug abuse, television addiction, jogging, immersion in rock music played on a Walkman, gambling, sex, Jazzercise, speaking in tongues, knitting, singing in the church choir, sponsoring a Little League baseball team, selling Amway products, practicing yoga, et cetera, et cetera *ad nauseam.* Almost any cause of enthusiasm may be trance-inducing. And for that matter, almost any lack of enthusiasm may be trance-inducing. Habitual unconsciousness may be harmful to one's well-being. But cults scarcely have the monopoly on habitual unconsciousness which Clark suggests. Further, I am amazed to note that Clark developed his theory on the basis of a small statistical sample. He states in his article, "The Manipulation of Madness," in which his theory is fully elaborated, that he had examined "50 individuals" in a four-year span. In addition, I note that although Clark credits cults with all sorts of devastation to the central nervous system, he has not hospitalized a patient in years.

IS THIS BRAINWASHING?

The issue of "brainwashing" is bound to surface. Although Clark prefers the term "mind control," it is clear that he considers brainwashing and the process of maintaining a dissociative state to be synonymous terms—a position which he elaborates in his paper "The Manipulation of Madness." I would agree with one of Clark's critics, Lieutenant Colonel Ralph C. Wood, USMC retired, who during his twenty-two years of active duty closely examined the "brainwashing" techniques practiced by the Chinese, North Koreans, and North Vietnamese. In response to Dr. Clark's 1977 testimony before the Vermont legislature Lieutenant Colonel Wood states: "Dr. Clark strongly implies that 'cult' religions use brainwashing techniques to convert and hold their followers when actually the techniques he describes are NOT brainwashing and to label them as such is a dangerous encroachment on basic liberties." Wood elaborates: "It is important to understand that these terms (reform, pressures, lectures, lies, etc.) alone do NOT constitute the practice of brainwashing. Brainwashing is defined by Webster's Dictionary as 'the forcible application of prolonged and intensive indoctrination . . . to induce someone to give up basic . . . beliefs and to accept contrasting regimented ideas.' Force is a very necessary element of the term and must be present at the initial entrance point, throughout the restraint period, *and* in the application of the indoctrination. There are degrees of force, of course, but the force required to justify the label 'brainwashing' must be either totally overwhelming physical force or brutal, violent actual life-threatening force."

It is my opinion that when Clark uses the terms "brainwashing" and "mind control," he is speaking of the application by groups of personal or psychological influences. It must be carefully noted that it is the groups as much as the influences of which Clark does not approve. Hence, it is the case in Clark's system that prolonged dissociation is always harmful and that a simple conversion to a group or belief unacceptable to Clark is evidence of prolonged dissociation and mental disequilibrium.

Clark frequently uses the term "mind control" to refer to the maintaining of a dissociative state. This term, which I have found totally useless in my work, is blatantly ambiguous. It suggests images both of the Manchurian Candidate and of those who program and control such automatons. The "puppet" may be said to be "under mind control" and his master to be "employing mind control." Clark often uses a second sense of "mind control"—i.e., a state induced in a subject by an artful and designing person as the result of which the subject controls his own thoughts so that they are invariably in conformity with the dicta of the manipulative individual or individuals. Since I know of no such total control in the noncult field of everyday reality, I find it impossible to ascribe such awesome power to cult recruiters. Behavior may be prescribed, attitudes influenced, beliefs affected, one's perception of reality distorted, but the mind cannot be controlled. No matter how submissive the individual is to the authority of the group, human consciousness retains a "mind of its own." It accepts our discipline only so long and then it goes where it goes and no one can control it. In whatever sense it is used by Clark, the term "mind control" strikes me as a dangerous exaggeration.

INFORMATION DISEASE AND SUDDEN PERSONALITY CHANGE

The most influential (and to date the sole) book-length exposition of the hypothesis that cults use brainwashing which can only be reversed by deprogramming is *Snapping* by Flo Conway and Jim Siegelman.[10] If Lifton's *Thought Reform and the Psychology of Totalism* is deprogramming's Bible, *Snapping* is its Summa Theologica, Constitution, and Encyclopaedia Britannica all rolled into one! Written in a style which, in my opinion, alternates between racy purple prose and cumbersome scientific-journalese, it is replete with tales of "America's epidemic of sudden personality change" (the book's subtitle). A quotation from the back cover of the paperback edition captures the flavor of the work:

> Hare Krishna chanters, est graduates, Moonies, Born Again converts . . . Charles Colson, Eldridge Cleaver, Patty Hearst, "Son of Sam"—What can they all possibly have in common?
>
> The answer is "snapping"—the term Flo Conway and Jim Siegelman use to describe the sudden drastic alteration of personality that has become an American phenomenon in the past decade and is spreading fast.* According to Conway and Siegelman, snapping is visible among religious-cult members, today's popular self-improvement mass therapies, and even within the vast Evangelical movement. The authors point out that mind-altering techniques employed by these groups tamper with the kind and quality of information fed to the brain—through isolation, repetition of chants, monotonous music, intimate touching, lack of sleep, physical duress, and fatigue. All of these tactics seriously affect the brain's ability to process information and may result in impaired awareness, irrationality, disorientation, delusion, and even violently destructive acts. The most horrifying example of this potential—the People's Temple massacre of November 1978 . . . calls for ways to control this very real threat to the future mental health of our society.

To summarize Conway and Siegelman, there is an epidemic of a new disease—an "informational disease"—a disorder in the way in which the brain processes information. It is evoked

* The term "snapping" is used by Ted Patrick and other deprogrammers to refer not only to sudden conversion but to sudden deconversion. When the cultist becomes aware that he has been had by the cult leader's brainwashing, he is said to have snapped, "like a light switch being turned on."

by stilling the mind, placing one's intellect on hold, and numbing it through any of a wide variety of ecstatic or blissful states. This newly discovered "mental illness," which has previously gone unnoticed by the mental health establishment, causes extreme weight gain or loss, abnormal skin conditions, menstrual dysfunctions in women, high-pitched voices and lack of facial hair in men, fear, guilt, hostility, depression, sexual dysfunction, violent outburst, suicidal tendencies as well as disturbed awareness, perception, and memory and impairment of the capabilities of the brain itself.

Talk about brainwashing! Any practice which gets one out of ordinary, self-directed, semi-attentive, means-to-an-end consciousness can cause brain damage. And consider the social implications. Conway and Siegelman remind us that there are over eight thousand new techniques for expanding human awareness and six million meditators and over three million converts to one thousand active religious cults and hundreds of thousands of born-againers. Surely our already overburdened mental health hospitals will be unable to handle the influx. So what is the solution? Deprogramming, of course. But not just by any deprogrammer. *Snapping* is an uncritical, reverential endorsement of Ted Patrick. It overstates his accomplishments, disparages his competition, and includes his address.

Depending on one's point of view, *Snapping* is the most helpful or disastrous account of cultism ever published. Or both. In quasi-scientific garb with its endless references to cybernetics and communication theory, it offers an explanation of a raft of troublesome experiences. And it does a masterful job of providing illustrations of conversion phenomena —secular as well as spiritual. In addition, it provides concerned parents with a sense that they are not alone, that there are thousands of others as confused as they.

But whatever the merits of *Snapping*, its overall effect has been insidious. For it popularizes the notion that if your progeny adopt a lifestyle at variance with your values, then it may safely be inferred that your offspring are suffering from a mental illness and that you have the right and the obligation to

have them kidnapped and deprogrammed, preferably by Ted
Patrick. Notice also how the Conway-Siegelman jeremiad
spreads from religious cults to the human potential movement
to est to the Manson family to the Son of Sam to evangelical
Christians to television viewing. And observe the Conway-
Siegelman distrust of intensity. Anything which reaches above
the threshold of boredom is suspect. Obviously there is a
whole lot of brainwashing going on, and very little of it by the
handful of religious sects routinely lambasted by the ACN.

BRAINWASHING WITHOUT CULTS

According to the current ACN perspective, brainwashing
rather than cultism is the problem. And deprogrammers are
the only interventionists qualified to deal with this difficulty. Is
it any wonder that deprogrammers are regularly sought out
whenever there is a frustrating or bewildering family problem?
Or when young adults report enthusiasm for any intense and
satisfying new experience, cause, or love? I still remember the
first client who told me that her daughter, who was in no way,
shape, or form involved in a cult, had been brainwashed and
that she should be deprogrammed. We will call the mother
"Nancy" and the daughter "Tami." At the time Nancy contacted me, her daughter was seventeen and living with her
twenty-three-year-old boyfriend, "Ed," and her boyfriend's
parents, "John" and "Sally." Nancy was convinced that her
daughter had been brainwashed because the formerly perfect
child had "never done anything like this before." Nancy
claimed that John, a respectable hypnotherapist, and his son
constituted a cult and that they had mesmerized Tami into
sexual promiscuity and pot smoking. Nancy had phoned every
deprogrammer, ex-cultist, ACNer, and cult-concerned professional she was able to locate. But the Bay Area ACN wanted
nothing to do with her. After hearing her story for the eighth
time, I offered to mediate. An appointment was arranged for
Nancy, Tami, and Ed. I had prepared a simple compromise to

defuse the situation. Nancy agreed in advance that if Tami would take a one-month vacation trip to Europe which the two had been planning for years, she would consider Tami an "emancipated minor" and would no longer interfere with her life. Tami agreed and I thought we were home free. But Ed, who in personality was a mirror image of Nancy—hysterical, self-centered, and pathologically anxious—vetoed the arrangement. There was no way that he would trust Nancy to keep her bargain and no way that he would sacrifice Tami's company for a month. My irritation with Ed was poorly concealed.

After four or five one-hour phone calls from Nancy, I heard nothing for two years, when I happened to run into Nancy at a meeting of a northern California anticult group. Her body language and tone of voice reeking with "I told you so," she proudly announced that her daughter had been deprogrammed by Joe Alexander, Jr., and that she was now living with relatives in another state. The deprogramming had been very difficult, she added, due to the sophisticated depersonalizing methods and the clever hypnotic techniques used by John. In the end her daughter had "snapped" and become normal again. The only problem was that she was still terribly depressed, which Nancy attributed to the posthypnotic suggestions which had been implanted by John. The last I heard of Nancy, she was participating in deprogrammings, providing her home as a place of confinement during the initial stages.

It is an unusual week when I do not receive a request to arrange the deprogramming of a truant or a doper or a punk rocker or a straying wife or a former lover or a schizophrenic or an AWOL marine or a newly wed or a recluse or a daughter who never visits or a witch or a psychic or a woman about to give birth attended only by a midwife or someone who is about to receive the proceeds of a trust fund or a homosexual or an advocate of the abolition of the death penalty or a daughter who works in a natural-food store which rents hot tubs. The list may sound comic, but the irony is that despite my advice parents went ahead and arranged deprogrammings in almost every one of these cases!

"But, Dr. Streiker," the reader will protest, "surely you are mistaken. Even hot-tub rental agents have rights. Surely the police and the courts would never countenance a rash of snatches." About one deprogramming in a thousand leads to serious legal consequences. A deprogrammer caught in the act runs virtually no risk of imprisonment. Once the specter of cultism or brainwashing is raised, police are loath to intervene and district attorneys are reluctant to prosecute. And what jury will convict sincere parents who are only motivated by love for their children and fear for their safety and mental well-being? There are frequent arrests and trials, both criminal and civil, to be sure. But parents who hire deprogrammers are more likely to be punished by exorbitant lawyers' fees than by prison sentences or monetary judgments.

For some time, deprogrammers have been moving out of the religious cult business and into family conflict resolution. The approach is simple: the family dispute is redefined in terms of brainwashing or hypnosis, and the snatch is ordered. And the beauty of the whole thing is that the accusation of brainwashing can never be disconfirmed. For everything which the subject does or says counts as proof of the accusation. Denials of brainwashing prove that the person is hypnotized. ("Of course you deny you're hypnotized. You have been programmed to deny you're hypnotized.") Admissions of brainwashing are seen as clever stratagems designed to catch the deprogrammer off guard. ("You're just pretending to agree with me so that I'll let you go back to the cult.") In other words, reminiscent of an earlier time, admit that you're a witch and die as a witch or deny that you're a witch and die as a witch. Contemporary philosophy defines as meaningless a statement which regards no evidence as counting against it. And that is how most assertions of brainwashing should be considered as well.

The issues which concern me as a counselor are conversion and fanaticism and what these imply. Unlike "brainwashing," conversion and fanaticism are not invisible mental processes but constellations of deeds, acts, and words. Vague, intangible mental states can never truly be changed because no one can observe them. How can we be sure that a cultist has been deprogrammed? Or that Ted Patrick has not brainwashed him? But through discussion, dialogue, persuasion, and moral example, conversion phenomena can be humanized and fanaticism can be moderated. The difference between deprogramming and this moderate approach is the difference between telling a story—no matter how entertaining that story may be —and telling the truth.

11

An Alternative
to Deprogramming

OBJECTIONS TO COERCION

Freedom Counseling Center was founded to provide a noncoercive and effective alternative to deprogramming. We are opposed to the kidnapping and forcible deconversion of cult members for several reasons. The following is a brief list of our major objections:

1. Adults have the right to make their own mistakes and to learn from them for themselves without parental intervention.

2. Deprogramming is unlawful, antinomian, and antisocial.

3. Deprogrammers employ no criteria for distinguishing between destructive cults and benign or beneficial groups—the accusation that a given group "uses mind control" or is "a destructive cult like the Moonies" is the only justification offered, and such argumentation is circular and specious.

4. Deprogrammers employ no criteria for distinguishing between destructive effects of a given group and benign or beneficial effects—no group/experience is entirely good or evil.

5. Deprogramming has become a means of asserting con-

trol on the behalf of relatively powerful family members over relatively powerless family members.

6. Deprogramming is based upon an explanatory model (brainwashing) which explains little and is problematic at best.

7. Deprogramming as a deconversion technique is of questionable effectiveness and is no more successful than less offensive methods.

8. Deprogramming is seldom required due to the transitory nature of most conversion phenomena and the relative ineffectiveness of most indoctrination.

9. The elasticity of the brainwashing or the "snapping" model encourages abuses. States of mind as well as patterns of behavior are too easily branded as psychologically detrimental so that forcible deconversion techniques may be applied in order to resolve interfamilial power struggles over a wide range of noncult issues.

10. Deprogramming often causes as many personality disorders as it cures.

11. Above all, deprogramming is a means of suppressing unpopular religious sects, social dissent, political causes, personal experimentation, romantic attachments, etc., and, as an instrument of social control, is alien to the philosophical/legal foundations of our society.

It may further be argued that deprogramming is counterproductive. The unsuccessfully deprogrammed convert becomes the true believer. The successfully deprogrammed convert becomes an object lesson to the faithful—the sinful world of your past is seductive and ruthless; your former friends and earthly family are not to be trusted. It is my observation that more converts are kept in cults and sects by fear of deprogramming than by any lasting benefit experienced in the group. As member after member is torn away from the group, deprogramming heightens the excitement of belonging to a fringe group; transforms paranoia into reasonable fear; provides a tangible and often encountered enemy in contrast to whom the recruit has a defined identity; justifies the rebellious young adult's desire to divorce himself from his family and their expectations; and attracts friends and supporters for the "persecuted minority" from among civil libertarians, established religions, and the media. Resisting deprogramming has become a test of strength and a badge of merit in many groups. The escapee is proudly introduced to new members and visitors from the outside. His determination demonstrates not only his own dedication but the validity of the group and its message.

OPPORTUNITY FOR REEVALUATION

During the last five years, Freedom Counseling Center has persuaded many young people to leave cults, and has done so without kidnapping them, holding them against their will, or subjecting them to stress-overload techniques. Obviously our approach differs from that of Ted Patrick and the deprogrammers who follow in his train.

Deprogrammers and Freedom Counseling Center deal with the same situation: young adults becoming involved with cults and surrendering the right to make their own decisions. But, according to the deprogrammers, cult members have *lost* their free will and they need to be *rescued*. Patrick and his followers have developed a coercive approach—that is, the cult member is kidnapped, bodily removed from the cult, and is berated into "thinking for himself." In practice, this means engaging in some sort of *counter-recruitment*. The deprogrammer rather than the cult now controls the milieu, secludes the individual, exploits his insecurities, employs harassment and fear, uses peer pressure (by forcing the cultist to listen to the testimony of apostates from his group) and humiliation to get the individual not only to defect from the group but to become an enemy of the group. One of my clients was deprogrammed from the Way International and was immediately put to work as the getaway driver during a "snatch." Within days of leaving a group which, he was told, was evil because it took the law into its own hands, here he was assisting a hired kidnapper take the law into his own hands. The experience left the ex-cultist profoundly shaken, confused, and depressed.

At Freedom Counseling Center we use no coercion, do not violate the law or our client's civil rights, and do not humiliate the convert. To summarize our approach in a few sentences: We begin with family counseling through which we discover whose problem we are really dealing with—that of overanxious parents or of a son or daughter who may have gotten in over his or her head. After assessing the family dynamics, accumulated misunderstandings, poor communications, and hostilities that have contributed to the present problem, we develop a strategy and assign roles to the estranged spouses, parents, family members, or friends. We make it the job of family members or friends to establish contact, develop trust, and create opportunities for dialogue. Where it is appropriate, staff members enter this dialogue and provide the cult recruit with their unique perspective. We offer cult members the opportunity to hear another other side of the story. We help them gain a perspective from which they can judge their experience for themselves. When I first meet them, they are so immersed in what they are doing that they have no objectivity. But every day they hear a still, small voice which asks them if they really know what they are doing, if they really want to continue. Many cultists do not give me an opportunity to say more than a few words, interrupting me with a question such as: "Do you think that God would be angry with me if I stopped lying to strangers to get them to give money to my group? I really hate what I'm doing and want to get out." And I give them permission to leave.

THE MEANING OF FREEDOM

The name of the agency which I direct incorporates the word "freedom," and our stated goal is to assist individuals in accepting responsibility for their own lives. Our conception of freedom is simple and basic. Freedom is the power to decide, and to accept responsibility for one's decisions. The human will is never free of influences. We are all coerced to a significant degree by our memories, upbringing, education; by the responses and expectations of those with whom we interact; and by the society in which we find ourselves. A free person is one who amid all the circumstances which condition and limit his freedom, sees the difference between necessary and unnecessary influences, and chooses which he will follow.

Freedom is responsible decision making—acting and accepting the consequences for one's actions. We support our clients and subjects in overcoming the undue and unfair influences of mind-bending by manipulative groups and persuasive individuals. And we are careful not to offer them one form of dependency in exchange for another. "Freedom counseling" is the process by which we challenge unexamined assumptions and stimulate a shift in perception which enables our subjects to tell the truth about themselves and awaken from their trance states. As Arthur J. Deikman, M.D., relates, the word "trance" in its technical sense refers "to the behavior of someone who has been hypnotized and is not responding normally."[1] In such a state, "awareness is restricted, attention is fixed, and behavior appears to be automatic, in response to suggestions and commands."[2] While it is often assumed that trance is a special or altered state of consciousness, it is in fact only a more intense instance of a state which is frequently experienced in ordinary life. According to Deikman's analysis, trance is a "loss of context," a state in which the individual's ordinary frame of reference is contracted. In addition to the fading of the individual's "generalized reality-orientation," trance is characterized by a certain amount of roleplaying. It has been noted by many students of hypnosis that the subject adopts the mannerisms of hypnotized persons as they are perceived in our society. The hypnotized subject acts as if he were an automaton because he knows that is how he is expected to act. Deikman explains that the subject is unconsciously motivated by the desire to please and win the approval of the father figure, the hypnotist, by fulfilling the hypnotist's wishes—whether these wishes are stated or implied.

We are all susceptible to the trance state—if not as hypnotic subjects, then in the "trance of everyday life"—because we long to be dependent upon a strong figure who will comfort, protect, and guide us while freeing us from the responsibility for our own acts. This predisposition to respond compliantly to suggestions which are heard "in the context of a dependency fantasy" makes us susceptible daily to hypnosis by individuals, social institutions, the government, the media, advertising, etc. For we are really responding automatically to the internalized parental figures whose love, acceptance, praise, and approval we crave. Beneath the level of our awareness, we are influenced by automatic, involuntary programming which tends to exchange conformity for security.[3]

Most of our lives are lived in a trance state, a sleep of fantasy, which is governed by our unconscious openness to being controlled. From time to time, we are awakened, snapped out of our trance, and brought into a state of acute awareness. As Werner Erhard has remarked: "The point is to be *de*hypnotized. That is what an *expanded* state of consciousness actually involves. This is a state of consciousness characterized by freedom, one in which one is not . . . [affected by] suggestions, beliefs, patterns, or any other unconscious or mechanistic force."[4] Sometimes we are shaken out of our sleep by intense experiences; sometimes by exposure to a charismatic individual; at other times by encountering an idea or insight which changes our way of perceiving ourselves. The skilled psychotherapist may be instrumental in the dehypnotizing of his client. Deikman finds that in psychiatry,

> . . . it is possible to bring into awareness [the patient's] . . . controlling fantasy, freeing the observing self from the area in question. With the increased freedom the automatized compliance and the trance associated with the fantasy can be broken. The result is closer contact with immediate reality, heightened perception of surroundings and people, and increased satisfaction in daily existence. The patient may describe the change as "waking from a dream."[5]

"Freedom counseling" is quite similar. We attempt to wake client and subject alike from the trance of their everyday lives. The parent who seeks our services on behalf of a "brain-washed mindless robot" who was a perfect son or daughter, until the evil group wrested away the subject's free will, needs to be aroused from slumber—if anyone does. Such clients need to be guided by the counselor into reexamining their assumptions about the cult or sect in question and setting aside myths, exaggerations, and hysteria. They must be urged to reevaluate their presuppositions about their children and about themselves as parents. And they must be trained to listen to their child, to abandon approaches which widen the gap between themselves and the convert. (For example, guilt-tripping—"Do you know what you're doing to your mother and me? How can you do this to us?"—and insults—"How can you be so stupid? What's wrong with you?"—are frequently attempted by parents but seldom lead to reconciliation.)

And the subject who has sold his selfhood for easy answers and group acceptance needs to be brought out of his trance as well. How do we wake him? First, we win his attention by listening attentively to his account of spiritual renewal, psychological breakthroughs, and personal revivification. We respond in a way that indicates our support for his spiritual aspirations. This is not merely a tactic—we are deeply interested, and we offer a brief sketch of the history of that interest. We indicate our respect for the subject's personal gains. But we critically examine the attribution of these gains to any group or charismatic person.

After giving the subject ample opportunity to relate his or her experiences in the group, my usual approach is to tell a cult member: "Eighty percent of what you are involved in is good, honorable, true, but twenty percent is manipulative, dishonest, and morally unacceptable." I urge the cult recruit to ask himself, "Do you really want to swallow that twenty percent?" We inform the cultist that there are many things taught by the cult which are true, but the real question is "whose truths are these?" When we encourage cult converts to express what they have learned, they often discover that they have always known these truths and that they do not require the structure of the group with its dishonesty and restrictive control in order to support their commitment to these truths. This approach allows the convert to leave with dignity, to tell himself: "I wasn't so stupid after all. Most of what they told me was true. I have learned something important that will remain with me for the rest of my life."

As the conversation progresses, we try to facilitate the reconstruction by the subject of an alternative explanation of his experience. We present our impressions of his family history and continuing dynamics, the unresolved tensions in the subject's life which led him to the group, the value and significance of the group as seen from a perspective other than that of the group, etc. Above all, we explain the concepts of obedience to authority and conformity as explicated by the research of Asch and Milgram. An understanding of the dynamics of obedience and conformity have led our subjects to more sudden "Aha!" experiences than hours of listening to atrocity tales. Further, scare stories from defectors and critics are fundamentally depressing in their effect upon potential defectors. But when subjects grasp the true character of the mind-bending games used by the group, they feel liberated and invigorated. From our point of view, we explain, "What you have undergone is familiar and valuable. However much of your explanation overlooks certain common facts about religious experience, group dynamics, and above all, about you." What I consciously try to do is offer the subject a basis for an alternate autobiography—one which places control in the hands of the subject and reduces the religious community to an instrument of self-revelation rather than the possessor of a monopoly on God's truth.

Ninety percent of those with whom we have spoken over the past five years have left authoritarian groups. We know of only one case where the subject later returned to the group; and in a second case, a subject joined another group, affording us a second opportunity to counsel him and his family. And we are able to arrange face to face meetings in about eighty percent of our cases—even with members of extremely paranoid and defensive groups. Our approach is not the only approach, and it will not "succeed" in every case. Some groups are simply too skillful in keeping their recruits away from friends, relatives, or counselors. And many converts will not be the least bit shaken in their newfound faith by exposure to our efforts. Nevertheless, the Center's approach is at least as successful as that of any deprogrammer. In virtually every case the Center has seen definite progress in the ability of family members to communicate with one another despite religious differences and in the self-critical manner in which both the cultist and concerned relatives or friends are able to view their own attitudes, values, and beliefs.

Since our purpose is mediation rather than deconversion, it has been somewhat of surprise to us that so many of our subjects decide to leave their new commitments as a result of the counseling process. We would feel that we had accomplished our goal if each party were able to communicate with and be heard by the other party. Often our role is buffer, translator, and megaphone. We receive the clichés, jargon, preconceptions, and prejudices of one party—e.g., cultist or parent—and reformulate them in the language of the other party. Whenever we detect an unwillingness to listen, we repeat, rephrase, and reassert the position of the unheard party until the communication is acknowledged. In the process, we absorb and deflect a considerable amount of disrespect, cynicism, and hostility.

We present our version of the truth about the group, the family and the individual. We offer a picture of a hopeful future without dependencies either upon the group or Mom and Dad. And, hopefully, we provide a perspective drawn from our explication of religious experience and social processes through which the subject is able to reevaluate his experience and his relationship with his loved ones. Often we introduce our subjects to former members of the same group whose cult and post-cult history has a profound influence on the subject's deliberations. At the conclusion of our discussions—which may last an evening or a week—we promise our continuing interest and support. No matter what the immediate outcome may be, we attempt to leave the door open to further dialogue. And then we withdraw.

Most of our subjects never return to the group. Some do, are unable to accept the inconsistencies and high-pressure tactics of the group, and leave shortly thereafter. Many have reported to us that upon their return they experienced a sense of disequilibrium which forced them to reconceptualize their beliefs and change their behavior—even though they chose to continue. Several in this category have been ostracized by the group for their "selfishness," "disobedience," and "negativity."

To the subject who is unsettled by what we have said but cannot decide who is telling the truth—the group or the counselor—we suggest a simple test: "Ask yourself," we urge, "what does the group want of you and what do we want? They want your entire life. We want nothing. So why should we lie?" Considering the defenses which fanatic groups erect against "satanic" outsiders, "worldly" influences, "negative" individuals, and "faith breakers," how is it that we are able to arrange so many voluntary sessions? I think the answer lies in recognizing that many converts want to be heard, understood, and appreciated by their loved ones. And so they take chances and defy the direct orders of the group. Second, many converts are ambivalent and want to hear "the other side," if only to resolve doubts so that they may increase their commitment to the group. Third, many converts desperately require and seek attention—whether it is from their parents or a parent substitute such as myself. Their involvement with the group functions much like a suicide attempt. It focuses family caring and financial resources on the previously ignored member.

Finally, many times we are able to arrange our encounters because the convert is not well suited to the group and the group is not well suited to the convert. Many recruits send off constant "rescue me" signals to family and friends—indications of frustration with the group, loneliness, nostalgia for old relationships, etc. There is a honeymoon phase, which generally lasts for about six months. During this stage, the convert is lured, indoctrinated, and reinforced through affection, approval, and praise. Soon positive reinforcement gives way to humiliation, threatened withdrawal of approval, and punishments. At this point, many converts grimly persevere, secretly hoping that someone will assume authority over them and give them permission to leave.

TWO PEERS REBEL

Not only do the above factors explain why our subjects willingly meet with us despite warnings of kidnapping, torture, and spiritual devastation, but these considerations also explain what motivates our subjects to defect. In sum, they have wanted out for some time. Our interchange brings this desire into the open and provides new peers who condone and support their decision. What we see at work in our counseling is an illustration of the essential dynamics of conformity to a group and of rebellion against that authority. Elsewhere in these pages we referred to the experiments of Solomon Asch on conformity and of Stanley Milgram on obedience to authority. Both conformity and obedience represent the abdication of responsibility and initiative to an external source.[6] However, as Milgram notes, the effects of each are significantly different. The obedient person accepts the authority of another, regarding the other as his superior, as one entitled to give orders. In this respect, the obedient subject does not imitate or identify with the superior. Usually it is quite clear to the subject what is expected by those seen as being in authority. Subjects embrace obedience and offer it as a defense when their actions are criticized. "I was only doing what I was told," they explain.[7]

The conformist, on the other hand, is motivated by his desire to fit with his peers. The conformist regards himself as a free agent. Although his behavior is in imitation of the group and corresponds with group expectations, the conformist often can neither see nor admit that his behavior is in any way influenced by theirs. It may be said that groups are more mind-bending than are charismatic leaders. We are conscious of our decisions vis-à-vis leaders but unconscious with regard to our group-induced compliance. In an attempt to explain this contrast between the obedient person and the conformist, Milgram states: "Because conformity is a response to pressures that are implicit, the subject interprets his own behavior as voluntary. He cannot pinpoint a legitimate reason for yielding to his peers, so that he denies he has done so, not only to the experimenter but to himself as well. In obedience the opposite is true."[8] In cults and sects, both motivations are pronounced. The member has little sense of accountability for his acts because they are directed by a higher authority. Yet he sees his being in the group and remaining with the group as acts of his free will. (Among Jonestown survivors whom I have counseled, it is customary for the individual to attribute his evil acts while in the group to the agency of Jim Jones, "the master manipulator," and to recall the group with fondness and nostalgia as "the most wonderful human beings who ever lived.")

Perhaps it is possible to take advantage of the tendency to conform to the expectations of peers by providing peers who resist authority rather than those who reinforce it. In the Milgram experiments, two thirds of the subjects obeyed the orders of the authority figure (the experimenter) and administered shocks well into the danger zone. But what if we were to surround the subject with peers who defied the experimenter. Milgram designed just such an experiment, entitled "Two Peers Rebel." In this version, the subject and two other "subjects," who are really confederates of the experimenter's, sit together at the control panel. At level 10 (150 volts, a "strong shock"), the first confederate refuses to comply and moves to the back of the room. The experiment and the administration of progressively stronger shocks continue. At shock level 14 (210 volts, a "very strong shock"), the second confederate refuses to comply. Does the subject ignore them and continue to obey the authority figure? No. In the group setting, 90 percent of the subjects defied the experimenter. Why the vast disparity? Milgram offers the following explanations:

1. The defiance of peers instills the idea of defiance.

2. The defiance of peers suggests that it is acceptable to defy.

3. The defiance of peers defines compliance as improper, confirming the subject's misgivings.

4. The continuing presence of the peers in the laboratory is experienced by the subject as social disapproval.

5. The refusal of the peers to cooperate forces the subject to face his own responsibility. Their withdrawal from the experiment puts the whole burden of responsibility on him.

6. The subject observes that the consequences of refusal to comply are minimal.

7. The power of the experimenter is diminished in the eyes of the subject by his failure to keep the two rebels in line.[9]

Milgram reports that the disobedience of the subjects was not without psychological cost. They felt that they had let the experimenter down, had failed to keep their word, had ruined the experiment, etc. Milgram finds: "The price of disobedience is a gnawing sense that one has been faithless. Even though he has chosen the morally correct action, the subject remains troubled by the disruption of the social order he brought about, and cannot fully dispel the feeling that he deserted a cause to which he had pledged support. It is he, and not the obedient subject, who experiences the burden of his action."[10]

What struck me as I read Milgram's words after I had counseled more than one thousand families was how well they fit my own observations. Without knowing it, Freedom Counseling Center has been re-creating "Two Peers Rebel" for years. First, the group induces conformity. Then we instill rebellion. The steps are as follows: Many cults and sects use a shill technique, teaming the new potential recruit with one or more experienced members and intentionally isolating the recruit from other potential converts. The subject complies with his pseudo-peers and is unable to reinforce his own misgivings through communication with those who share his ambivalence. The conformity is implicit; the justification, if required, is that he is acting of his own free will and in obedience to the freely accepted authority of his superior or leader.

What disrupts this cleverly managed abdication of freedom? The resurfacing of the suppressed and unresolved ambivalence as well as exposure to a new group situation—the group now consisting of counselors, friends, former members, and family. Consider the dynamics of the new group—their non-acceptance of the cult or sect; their defiance of the cult or sect; and the fact that they remain relatively sane, normal, and well adjusted despite their defiance of the divine will as interpreted by the cult or sect. If ex-members are involved in the counseling, as they are in half my cases, they demonstrate that the consequences of defection are minimal and that the power of the cult or sect is not absolute. In fact, many cults and sects induce the phobia that if the convert ever leaves the group he will die a horrible death within weeks, go insane, be destroyed by evil spirits, or otherwise be punished by God. The mere existence and presence of an ex-member is a powerful inducement to doubt the cult or sect.

But as successful as this approach is at dislodging converts from authoritarian groups, it is costly to the convert. For weeks or months, he may feel disoriented, guilty, embarrassed, isolated, angry, and depressed. Freedom is often painful. Restoring a sensitive individual to a world of risk, contingency, hurt, and decision is not to be taken lightly. The defector has many needs. His decision to leave the authoritarian group is not a finished product or an end in itself. If there is not adequate follow-up and well-planned rehabilitation, the result can be a disaster. The defector needs to be reconnected to nurturing and supportive experiences, to caring and compassionate persons, and to a process of self-evaluation and growth which moves him from the limbo of the ex-member identity to a self-actualizing state of being. The process which we recommend is applicable not only to the defector as a means of restoration; it is a prescription for enhancing the freedom of those who have never joined a cult or sect.

PROGRAMMING FOR FREEDOM

When a subject decides to leave an authoritarian group, we urge him to state the "truths" that he has learned in the group and consciously to make them his own. We also instruct our subject in how to appropriate the conformity-inducing techniques of the group as a means of personal transformation. In other words, if the cult or sect can take advantage of the individual's susceptibility and program him for their purposes, why should the individual not be able to adapt their techniques in order to program himself for success?

In an earlier chapter, we delineated a sixteen-step process used by cult groups to elicit "sudden personality change." And we have stated our conviction that these procedures may be used by the client in pursuit of his own purposes as well as by groups to further their own ends. We observed that first cults change behavior, that changes in behavior elicit changes in attitudes, that changes in attitudes produce changes in beliefs, and, finally, changes in beliefs lead to changes in feelings. But cannot this "technology of mind control" be utilized as a "technology of self-control"? Enhancing freedom requires that we liberate ourselves from old scripts, discredited beliefs, self-destructive patterns of behavior, undesirable automatic or mechanistic forces, our negative self-image, and whatever else binds us to the hurts, narrowness, and smallness of the past. Would not the elements of self-control be similar to those just enumerated? What I am suggesting is that we take charge and create our own artificial atmosphere for self-transformation. We will need to nourish our own child-nature, indulging ourselves occasionally in non-utilitarian play activities "just for fun." We will have to risk suspending judgment and accepting ourselves and others, lowering the barriers to self-knowledge and intimacy. We will have to bombard ourselves with the enjoyment of ourselves, rigidly scheduling the time for the processes of self-discovery, inundating ourselves with new ideas and new experiences, disrupting old routines and habits.

Each of us should be our own theologian and ethicist, creating our own structured and dovetailed system of truths. There are many paradigms available from religious thinkers, scriptures, the faith of our childhood, philosophers, novelists, poets, motivational and self-help writers, etc. So there is no need to reinvent the wheel but only to install it. We can each appeal to our own cherished authorities—even if they are only our wiser friends or our own best insights. A well-kept record of our own progress will soon add significance and dignity to our own system.

Other instructions which I would suggest to those who wish to adopt a technology of self-control: Change your pattern of behavior—dress differently, get a new haircut, attend a different church, pursue a neglected hobby, read a book that you have never found time for, or see a movie that you missed in your youth (video cassette recorders and tapes of movies are available for rental in most communities). Take a college course dealing with something which has always interested you. Do a dozen things that you desire and value. Those actions will generate attitudes, beliefs, and feelings.

Create your own community. Deliberately surround yourself with persons who reinforce your most hopeful, creative moments and who experience you as supportive of theirs. And withdraw from persons and circumstances which needlessly depress, suppress, limit, restrict, or inhibit you. Listen to your own thoughts, monitor your own responses. Negativity is a bad habit. Let go of guilt, resentment, and self-righteousness. The past is the past. Plan, promote your plans, persevere in your plans. Then evaluate your progress in concrete terms, refine, replan, and go on.

Put your faith into action. If you believe something, share that belief. Support the hopes of others. Involve yourself in your community. Apply your faith to the real issues of our times—however you define them. Above all, keep your word. For the failure of individuals, groups, businesses, and governments to honor their promises is the most destructive force at work in our society today. Conversely, a restoration of a sense of honor and commitment—doing what we have said we would —is the surest hope for our own well-being or for the sanity of our world. Live as if each act is important. For it either expresses the purpose for which we live or it reveals the emptiness of our existence. The choice is ours to make. And that is, after all, the meaning of freedom.

For the purpose of our recommended program, we define freedom as the ability to choose responsibly—that is, to determine what one wants, to determine how to get it, and then to get it. Enhancing one's freedom is the process of stimulating the ability to transform one's situation from undesirable to desirable. It is the process of realistically defining what one wants and how to obtain it, of assessing the cost, and deciding whether one is willing to pay it. In the personal sphere, enhanced freedom is achieved by transforming oneself. In the interpersonal sphere it means transforming the quality of one's relationships with significant others so that these relationships are mutually fulfilling. In the social sphere, enhanced freedom means accepting responsibility for making the world work for everyone so that it works for the individual.

We have discovered that many of our clients suffer from a lack of desire. They have no concrete wants list. They do not feel that they deserve anything, so why should they have desires? We emphasize that desire is powerful in ungluing an individual from his state of depression, lethargy, and dependence. The free person knows what he or she wants. Until the individual develops an acute sense of goals, hopes, and dreams for himself, he will continue to be stuck. The first question, then, that each of us must answer is: What do I want?

Second, the attainment of one's own wishes requires a sense of a supportive world, of a moral order which rewards virtue, persistence, honesty, etc. I am not dictating a list of dos and don'ts. What I am suggesting is that each of us must come to grips with the questions: What kind of world do I want? As I pursue what I want, what must be true of reality in order for me to get it? At this point, each individual must develop his own list of moral or theological certainties about himself, his dealings with others, and the order of things.

Third, once serious attention has been directed to what one wants and the values which will govern one's behavior in seeking what one wants, the problem remains how to get from here

—one's present situation—to there—that which one desires. At this point, the magic of imagination comes into play. We encourage individuals to transform themselves by transforming their self-images. This is a lesson that this counselor learned from his clients. One of my clients who was grateful to me for the assistance which I provided her in untangling herself from a cult group became concerned at some of the ongoing problems which I faced in my work and gave me a book by Napoleon Hill, *Think and Grow Rich.* Another client recommended Maxwell Maltz's *Psycho-Cybernetics.* I used to be very skeptical of self-help books as facile and superficial, but I have found the insights and common sense of Hill and Maltz too helpful to be ignored.

To summarize Hill:

1. All achievement has as its source an idea freely created.

2. Ideas have an inherent tendency to transform themselves into reality.

3. Through techniques of active imagination, the individual is able to re-create his expectations and, hence, influence his everyday reality.

4. Active imagination is greatly enhanced and supported by surrounding oneself with the proper friends and acquaintances.

To summarize Maltz:

1. In order to stop taking the victim's position in life, it is necessary to accept responsibility for your self-image.

2. Begin by avoiding resentment, self-righteousness, and guilt. Such states fasten you to the past, prevent you from dealing with the present, and cause dissatisfaction. What has happened, has happened. Do not resist it.

3. Resentment, self-righteousness, and guilt create inhibition. Practice disinhibition. Do what you want to do despite your reticence, shyness, and fear of rejection. Success leads to success.

4. Create a positive self-image by placing yourself in a state of physical relaxation and actively, concretely imagining yourself as possessing the new self-image and all that accompanies it. Maltz suggests that we retreat into a room of the mind at

least thirty minutes a day. Imagine in vivid detail that we possess everything which we want—objects, relationships, honors, learning, etc. His conviction is that the nervous system cannot distinguish between an actual experience and one vividly imagined.

The state of relaxation may be attained by meditation (e.g., focusing on one's breathing while counting the breaths), "relaxation response," prayer, chanting, listening to calming music, taking a hot bath, walking in nature—or whatever works. The period of relaxation and the practice of active visualization must be regular and consistent—at least twenty minutes a day for three weeks. Maltz maintains that it takes twenty-one days for a new suggestion or positive self-image to take hold. I find it significant that most cult/sect recruitment observes a twenty-one- to forty-day period of indoctrination or advanced studies. They seem to know what Maltz has observed, that three weeks of concrete visualization of a new identity while in a relaxed or altered state enables the new suggestion to take hold in the individual's unconscious mind. The process of relaxation and suggestion is neither good nor evil. We can use it to allow ourselves to be robbed of our freedom or to deeply enhance our selfhood.

As we change our own self-image, we must also change our patterns of behavior. Getting what we want requires that we plan for it by setting goals, assessing resources, developing strategies, scheduling our time, and evaluating our progress. The style or format of goal setting and monitoring of progress is relatively unimportant as long as there is a conscious, deliberate, and articulated process.

However, desiring success and planning for it is useless without persistence. The results of everything which has been urged to this point must constantly be fed back into the visualization and self-imaging process. And the individual must establish his own supportive group. For without support, deliberation fades and good intentions are forgotten.

About three weeks into the process, the individual is encouraged to ask himself: Is it all really worth it? Do I still want what I set out for? For he must constantly renew his sense of what he wants, what he values, and his realization that he has taken charge, has accepted responsibility for his own self-image, his own life. As we have noted, each of us has a tendency to obey those who remind us of the inner father figure and to conform to the expectations of those who accept and love us. The self-training program which we recommend encourages a unique form of obedience and conformity. It challenges the individual to be his own parent and his own peers, and to accept responsibility for his own self-image and for the world which he chooses to live in. Of course, it is easier to allow an organized, manipulative group to seduce, indoctrinate, and control us. The processes which we have sketched require discipline, persistence, and imagination. They demand an awareness and a responsiveness which may prove positively taxing. Cults provide easy answers. Discovering and enjoying one's freedom is not a comfortable path. Only the truth which I find for myself can set me free.

THE WAY BACK

The new believers are among us. Their ideas are strange, their practices exotic, their beliefs obscure, their attitudes peculiar. They have become strangers who cannot be knit into the fabric of our communal expectations. Many respond to the new believers with fear, suspicion, and hostility. Anxious parents employ the services of coercive deprogrammers to forcibly "rescue" their adult children, detaining them until they can be persuaded to renounce their beliefs. Less extreme attempts to woo members of nontraditional communal groups back to self-determination are undertaken by counselors such as myself. More often than not the efforts of deprogrammers and other "exit counselors" will be successful. Further, thousands of cult members will voluntarily depart from their newfound allegiances. Of course, many a convert will remain among the faithful for years—even a lifetime. But a sizable number will experience a brief period of ecstasy followed by the all-encompassing emptiness of losing faith. It is these "new disbelievers" who concern me. For they are in desperate need of friends, guides, and counselors as they seek the way back.

LOSING FAITH

What are the emotional consequences of losing faith? Reactions include confusion, doubt, guilt, anxiety, ambivalence, and lack of direction. In sum, a loss of inner balance characterizes the former believer. Leaving a cult requires a leap of faith no less drastic then joining such a group. Whether the act of disavowal stems from a sudden disenchantment or from a gradual waning of loyalty, loss of faith may leave the individual embittered, humiliated, lacking in self-confidence, angry, and depressed. Disavowal triggers grieving reactions similar to those which follow divorce, the death of a spouse or other family member, a change of vocation, or the end of a love affair.

Many former disciples interviewed by the author report a mixed reaction of righteous indignation mingled with fear of having committed a fatal personal error. On the one hand, the ex-convert feels that he or she has been deluded, manipulated, and exploited by the sect and its leadership. On the other hand, the rebel expresses an anxiousness approaching panic: "Perhaps I am making a terrible mistake. God may be trying my faith. Satan may be tempting me. What have I done?" A common solution is a temporary compromise, living in a no-man's-land in which the doctrinal content of the deserted sect is still affirmed by the individual while the leadership or members of the group are rejected as hypocrites, traitors, heretics who have betrayed the "true faith." One of David Berg's first converts recently related to me her opinion that Berg had departed from the "fundamental Christianity" of the early days of the Children of God. Yet for a decade this disciple tolerated the transformation of Berg into "Moses David, God's last-day prophet" and the supplanting of revivalistic theology and morality with Berg's sexual laxity and his claims to be God's only true prophet, priest, and king.

Those who defect from the group because of their perception that the group has betrayed its own ideals may attempt to survive in reformed cells numbering from a handful to a righteous remnant of one or two. Numerous clients from the Church of Scientology and the Hare Krishnas come to mind. Since the righteous remnant is not as thoroughly disoriented as the utterly disenchanted, the loss of identity with its accompanying ennui, self-alienation, and confusion is less pronounced. More typical is a former Moonie whom I have tracked from the day he first encountered the covert evangelists of the Unification Church, through his conversion and career among the faithful, through his disenchantment, departure, and disavowal of the Church, until his present life in a locale and a lifestyle far removed from his days as a follower of the Reverend Sun Myung Moon. Today he praises the Moonies, respects the Moonies, despises the Moonies, fears the Moonies, belittles the Moonies. His defection is irrevocable and unconditional, but his utterances concerning the sect are irreconcilable. To admit total self-deception, to characterize the sect as solely evil, is to view oneself in a most negative manner—as a weak-willed dupe, a fool, a pawn. To grant too much value to the sect and its way of life is to raise the possibility that defection signifies grievous error, self-betrayal, or sloth. Hence, ambivalence is the best defense and the most comfortable psychological habitation.

Losing faith is like falling out of love. The rapturous sense of oneness disappears. The individual's feeling of isolation returns. The attachment to the beloved which enabled the lover to escape the finitude of a solitary ego has been sundered. "I am I, and you are you, and we shall remain divided." So the convert finds himself alone and less than totally perfected. He is anchored by circumstances and responsibilities to a mundane world that stubbornly refuses to disappear or accept redemption. Life is again difficult, awkward, and painful.

When faith no longer works, the former zealot has several choices:

  1. He may shrug his shoulders, accept the "benefits" gained from his time with the group, and return to his former life.

  2. He may counter-convert—that is, compensate for disappointed expectations by loving what he formerly shunned and hating what he previously adored. Most deprogrammers of my acquaintance are ex-cultists. And all too many ex-cultists can imagine no future career choices other than deprogramming.

  3. The former cultist may find a worthier object of his total devotion. Ex-cultists are particularly vulnerable to romantic involvements, holy causes, and heroes. Many of the pre-Jonestown defectors from the People's Temple were devotees of self-proclaimed psychics or fundamentalist Christianity when I first met them.

  4. The individual may become cynical—often to the point of nearly suicidal desperation.

  5. He may interpret his release from the group as the beginning of a period of creative freedom and boundless self-realization.

APPROACHES TO REHABILITATION

Various strategies are employed in rehabilitating the ex-cultist. Coercive deprogrammers present cult phenomena as radically evil and perverse. Their clients are taught that they are helpless victims who have been brainwashed, hypnotized, and otherwise deprived of their own wills. Deprogramming consists of forcing cultists to "think for themselves"—or so the deprogrammers maintain. It seems to me that their real goal is the induction of an emotionally traumatic experience—a catharsis culminating in the renunciation of the group. After the "rescue" of the individual from the cult, the next step is to secure his or her person from the machinations of the cult. Since cults are seen as wealthy, powerful empires which will stop at nothing to thwart the efforts of the deprogrammers,

rehabilitation necessitates holding the deprogrammee inc[
municado, with or without his or her permission, until the
deprogrammee passes through his or her period of "floating"
—that is, ambivalence and susceptibility to being reconverted
to the cult. Such incarceration at remote "secure" facilities is
expensive (about four thousand dollars per month), legally
and morally questionable, and frequently ineffectual. Also,
some "rehab" centers are heavily infused with fundamentalist
Christian ideologies which are just as unacceptable to Jewish
and Roman Catholic parents of their charges as the lifestyles of
the cults. Also, in a coercive and secretive atmosphere psychological, physical, and sexual abuses are not unknown. And
accountability, legal responsibility, quality control, and pro-
fessionalism are issues which can scarcely be addressed. Such
rehabilitation more often than not produces the counter-conversion negative identity mentioned above.

Usually there is no follow-up to deprogramming. Almost all
cultists persuaded to defect from groups in the Bay Area are
simply sent home—often to highly dysfunctional family situations. They report the following problems: depression, interpersonal awkwardness, lack of motivation, unrealistic career
expectations, poor nutrition, inability to concentrate, poor
impulse control, and extreme suggestibility. These ex-cultists
are gullible, undisciplined, inarticulate, and, above all, easy
marks—what Graham Greene has termed "murderees." They
are neither unintelligent nor unattractive—but incredibly naïve and impractical.

The rehabilitation of former cultists requires a supportive
yet confrontive familylike milieu. Our model at Freedom
Counseling Center emphasizes the following elements:
  a) high expectations
  b) rigid scheduling
  c) shared responsibilities
  d) transition
  e) departure
We believe that the high-expectations halfway-house model
offers the best approach to the rehabilitation of ex-cultists.
Our goal is the ongoing operation of a home for about eight

individuals, a daytime counseling director, and a nighttime/ weekend counselor. Wake-up and lights-out are strictly observed. The first item given to each client is an alarm clock. After breakfast all clients are required to depart the grounds until late afternoon unless they are participating in individual or group counseling. A daily schedule of educational, cultural, or vocational activities is prepared for each day by the client with the assistance of his or her counselor. Clients are responsible for laundry, household chores, and most meal preparation. Each client participates in at least an hour a day of one-to-one counseling as well as twice-weekly group counseling. The Center staff is supplemented by mental health professionals. Length of residence is usually three weeks and is limited to three months. The halfway house is not an anticult cult. It is a transitional existence and a place of refuge where the client knows that he can find friendly support after his "graduation." Ex-clients are welcome to Wednesday-night family dinner and rap sessions.

A fundamental principle of the program is its voluntary nature. No client is held against his or her will. No one is denied access to the mails or telephones. Clients may leave the program whenever they choose. Over the past five years such a program has been offered whenever there was a cluster of former members sufficient to require it. Clients have been from a number of groups, including Synanon, the Unification Church, the Children of God, the Divine Light Mission, the Christ Family, the Hare Krishnas, and the People's Temple. Not one individual served in this program has returned to a cult.

Helping clients on their way back requires insight, information, understanding, and *impatience.* We find that we must be able to provide affection and sympathy and be able to interpret the individual's experience through acquaintance with the ideology and dynamics of the particular group to which the client belonged. And yet our most important role is setting limits. "We are here to help you help yourself" is our message. "But we cannot help you despite yourself. So stop feeling sorry for yourself, stop blaming the group, your parents, the evil, materialistic world, or whatever, for your problems. The greatest evil is deliberate indecision—the decision to make no decisions—to let the cult or the counselor lead your life for you. Forget it. That's not why you are here. Tonight you will be having dinner with us. Next week or next month you will be inviting us to your apartment after a day at school or at your new job to have dinner with you. And we will tell everyone here how proud we are of you. For that, my friend, is all that we want."

METHODS AND RESULTS

Method number 1 (coercive deprogramming followed by involuntary rehabilitation) encourages self-doubt, dependence, negative formation, helplessness, and phobias. In addition, it is self-perpetuating, as today's deprogrammee becomes tomorrow's deprogrammer.

Method number 2 (coercive or persuasive deprogramming without rehabilitation) at best restores the client to his or her ambiguous pre-cult state and fate. At worst, it returns the individual to untenable, stress-laden circumstances from which life in a cult is a welcome escape.

Method number 3 (a high-expectations halfway house) grants dignity and responsibility to the individual by dispensing with coercion. At the same time the halfway house approach takes seriously the grave practical and emotional difficulties faced by the ex-cultist during his reentry. This model offers a high degree of safety and support during a period of readjustment. It validates personal goals based upon individual disposition rather than images grounded in anticult activities.

Method number 1 (coercive deprogramming/rehabilitation) is based on the notorious brainwashing model which sees individuals as totally stripped of freedom of choice by cult mind manipulation. Through the use of thought-reform tech-

niques to counteract the alleged use of thought-reform techniques, coercive deprogramming fights fire with fire.

Method number 2 (deprogramming without follow-up) is
based upon an exorcism model. "Once the devil has been
driven away by the power of God, he will not return. Once
saved, always saved." If the deprogrammee returns to the cult,
that means that he or she only faked being deprogrammed or
was so "brain-damaged" that the deprogramming was too
late. Ted Patrick claims a success rate of almost 100 percent.
His competitors (many of them his former associates) claim
that nearly half of his clients outwit him by feigning repentance
and subsequently go back to their respective cults.

Method number 3 (the high-expectations transitional milieu) is based on the assumption that even when subjected to
highly effective means of mind manipulation, human beings
retain the freedom to choose. I have seen young adults whose
minds were confused, whose bodies were exhausted, whose
nervous systems were strained almost beyond endurance, who
truly were the victims of unscrupulous groups that employed
deception, beatings, induced phobias, terror, sensory overload, and numerous forms of behavioral modification to
achieve their ends. But I have never yet had a client who could
convince me that he or she was only a pawn and not a partner
in the process of self-abnegation. I have spent a great deal of
time with defectors and survivors from Jonestown and none of
them accepts personal responsibility for the communal horror
in which they participated for six or eight or twenty years prior
to the jungle apocalypse. They tell me, "Jim Jones was a master manipulator. He brainwashed us. We were helpless victims.
There was nothing we could do. He totally controlled our
lives." Can I call these survivors of this fathomless holocaust
liars? Of course not. It would be heartless to blame the victims.
Yet these same individuals have confessed to me that while
members of the People's Temple they committed acts of violence, forgery, burglary, and worse—without any specific orders from Jim Jones. I wonder, at what point do pawns become
willing victims? And when is it possible to hold "victims" culpable for their own crimes?

But if I have learned anything in the years that I have spent counseling ex-cultists, it is that return to the mainstream—coping with the ambiguities, delights, and pains of human existence—is possible only for those who admit: "I was duped. I was abused. I was had. But I let it happen. I helped. I got what I wanted *then.*" And our work as counselors, friends, and guides is the transformation of memories of that bittersweet *then* into possibilities of a hope-filled *now.*

As I remarked above, the new believers are among us. So are the new disbelievers. What happens to the convert within a religious cult is a matter of personal predisposition, social expectations, the circumstances of setting, and the chemistry of combining an individual with a community of faith. No one can predict the outcome when such variables are involved. One convert will become a lifelong devotee. Another will fall away from a new faith within three months. A third will become a charismatic leader. A fourth will be an apostate. Yet another will put away all such matters as but another manifestation of an outgrown childishness. One convert will betray a former spiritual master to the mass media as a fraud, a thief, a seducer of the innocent. One will undergo a devastating and transforming experience which within a week will be rationalized and dismissed as autosuggestion within an atmosphere of group hysteria. And finally, one convert will write me and state, "What you say about all those demonic cults and their false leaders is so true. But if you could only experience what I have found through God's only prophet in his true church, you would know the way, the truth, and the life."

For as long as there is loneliness, as long as the difference between good and evil is a blur, as long as we feel unloved and incapable of loving, as long as our quest for personal significance is frustrated, as long as our search for the perfect community eludes us, the inner ear will strain to hear strange messengers, new gospels, whispers of hope, promises of utopia. Listen well—whether you regard their affirmations as cruel hoaxes or as revelations of God. The new believers cannot be ignored.

The new believers are coming. And the new disbelievers are not far behind!

12

❦❦❦

Can Anything Be Done?

CULTS AS A SCAPEGOAT

Before doing anything to protect our children and ourselves from the incursions of fanatic groups, we must recognize a basic fact. "Destructive cultism" is a scapegoat. The alleged sins of cults are the sins of society and of the family itself. We justly accuse cults of breaking up families, mind-bending, exploitation, replacing thoughts with clichés, requiring unquestioning obedience and total self-abnegation, making total demands and coercively enforcing them. If we examine our social realities and family circumstances at this time in history, we find that family disruption, personal instability, intellectual superficiality, exploitation of the powerless by the powerful, and recourse to coercive means, including violence, are all too common.

Conversion of a young adult to a cult or sect is *as disturbing* to many families as the following contingencies involving young adults:

—a mixed marriage,
—drug experimentation,
—relocation away from the family home,
—homosexuality,

—dropping out (e.g., refusing to take one's place in a family-owned business),
—penury and joblessness,
—divorce,
—deciding not to have children,
—a bizarre, health-threatening diet,
—pursuing a strange vocational choice (e.g., leaving law school to become a farmer or giving up a medical practice to become a hang-glide instructor),
—showing preference for one parent over the other after a parental divorce.

But what must be underscored is that having a child in a cult is *no more detrimental* to a family than any of the above.

Cults are a manifestation of and a minor contributory factor to some nasty and deep-seated problems. Every year, a few members of cults or sects commit suicide and a handful of fanatics act out their paranoid delusions to the bitter end—dying in a shoot-out with police or murdering an innocent victim or causing a death through negligence. Such behavior is intolerable. But, in all fairness, I must point out that the suicide rate among my clients/subjects who are involved in cults and the rate of their involvement in violent crime or self-destructive acts are negligible compared to the incidence of such things in the general population. America is the most violent industrialized nation on the face of the earth. Our prisons are filled to overflowing. An incredibly high percentage of our children will be physically and/or sexually abused before they reach adulthood. In a society in which suicide is second only to automobile accidents as a cause of death among young adults, we castigate a handful of poorly organized and marginally successful religious groups as though they were a major threat to the social order. At a time in which child abuse has "reached serious proportions,"[1] a coalition of clergy chooses to single out cults. Yes, fanatic groups are frustrating and threatening on a case-by-case basis. Yes, the attitudes of many cults and sects toward women and children are prehistoric. But let us not lose perspective.

Families have expectations regarding their children—even when those children become adults and have children of their own. These expectations are neither inventions nor the products of spontaneous generation. Conceptions of acceptable behavior, proper conduct, valuable careers, responsibility, and duty are cultivated by a society as though they are crops. Although the process is inefficient (since it is often characterized by waste, error, outmoded assumptions, inconsistency, and inadequate resources), it is supported by all the institutions of society, including government, education, and the churches. Families and the greater society can be quite coercive in enforcing their demands. When they encounter obstinate resistance, they call upon agencies of social control such as the police, social services, mental health professionals, and clergy to support them. In addition, without outside help they resort to guilt-tripping, intimidation, bribes, and other maneuvers to achieve their ends.

When the repertoire of options is exhausted, the family (as well as society to some extent) turns to extralegal and extraordinary agents of social control. But in order to do this, it is necessary to redefine the problem by projecting it upon dark and shadowy forces—e.g., destructive cultism. Seldom does conversion of a cult member instigate family dysfunctions, although it clearly exaggerates them. Accepting the "myth of the invasion of the body snatchers"—that is, that there are artful and designing persons who cause family disruptions by mentally kidnapping our innocent children through the application of the technology of mind control—may provide comfort and displace guilt. But, as we have attempted to demonstrate, the brainwashing hypothesis causes more problems than it solves. Invariably the introduction of the brainwashing explanation confuses the issues. Whenever I hear the term used as an explanation of patterns of behavior which one generation finds unacceptable in the next, I have come to suspect that what is really occurring is a power struggle between generations. In case after case of deprogramming and attempted deprogramming which I have examined, the desire to punish and the need to control stand out like a midnight bonfire on a hilltop.

Cult involvement, like all social problems, should be dealt with through preventive as well as ameliorative means. Yet most approaches to producing "cult awareness" are based on unexamined assumptions and on a failure to explore why cults thrive in this society at this time in its history.

WHY CULTS FLOURISH

Where there is widespread avoidance of responsibility, alienation, and lack of viable images for self-development, fanatic groups are sure to flourish. Such groups do not sit in wait to prey upon us with their superior strategies for mental domination. They are projections of our inadequacies. For example, we have noted that authoritarian groups have an underdeveloped sense of truthfulness. Even when it costs them nothing to tell the truth, many of their adherents will gladly lie. Since the ends to which they have committed themselves transcend human morality, they feel justified in massaging the truth to fit their needs. Did cults invent this morality of deception and distortion? Did they introduce the notion that the rules of everyday decency may be suspended if one finds them inconvenient? Not at all. They reflect the most serious shortage of natural resources faced by modern America: the scant supply of persons who will keep their word. Dealing with dishonesty and lawlessness within authoritarian groups is no more frustrating than dealing with the product which does not live up to its advertising, the repairman who replaces perfectly good parts, the surgeon who performs an unnecessary operation, the craftsman who never finishes the job, the client who receives goods or services and does not pay the bill, the salesperson who willfully conceals the defects of the product, the philanderer who expects his spouse to keep vows which he disregards, the builder who bribes an inspector so that he can get away with using substandard materials, the food processor who neglects to sterilize canned goods, the prosecutor who refuses to enforce the law, etc.

There is a tinge of hypocrisy in the outrage with which we regard cults. They deserve no praise for their lack of decency, honesty, or integrity. But neither do they deserve to be required to obey standards of conduct and responsibility that few of us observe. It is time that we accepted cults for what they are. They are not a blight, a national disgrace, or a social disease. They are more or less organized groups of religious believers who manifest all the inconsistencies, one-sidedness, and zeal of any new religious group. And they are not static forces against which we must align our troops. They are living and changing entities which either leave their immature excesses behind or die. Further, they are much less resistant to our responses than we imagine. In such groups are concentrated the best and the worst traits of our society and our patterns of parenting. In their own negative way, cults are dealing with the issues which the institutions of our nation have left to benign neglect: questions of personal and family stability; the morality of persuasive techniques in advertising, politics, and sales; the value of critical and independent thought; the need to humanize medicine and technology; and the distribution of wealth and power. The current dispute about cults and sects remains one of the few arenas in which such life-and-death issues appear. It should not take the return of the Dark Ages, which cult irrationality and magical thinking represent, to spur us to renew the foundations of our civilization. But if that is what it takes, then cults have rendered us a valuable service.

PROFILES OF CULT RECRUITS AND THEIR FAMILIES

Cults are substitute families. If the traditional family were functioning smoothly—meeting the needs of its members, communicating its values, establishing a sense of safety and security, providing emotional support, endowing new generations with a vision of a hopeful future—then there would be no role for the surrogate families provided by cults and sects. If there is a single factor which predisposes a young adult to join a cult, it is the lack of a family which works for him. Whether his family is as dysfunctional as he supposes, the fact is that the cult convert perceives it as having failed him.

It is remarkable to me how close to a certain stereotype or profile most of my cases fall. In other words, the generalities at which I have arrived about cult recruits and their families are statistical averages, but more of my clients and subjects conform to the average than deviate from it—which is significant. For in compiling an average based on any data, there is no particular likelihood that most of the instances will be nearly identical to the average. For example, the observation that the average age of the members of my Rotary Club is thirty-eight does not mean that even a single member of the club is between thirty-five to forty-one years of age.

We have described the typical cult convert above. I would add a few details to that depiction. The profile of the average cult recruit is as follows: white; from a suburban family; parents are still married to one another; twenty-two years of age; male (by a three to one ratio); three and a half years of college education; the second of three children; not a heavy drug user but has used marijuana occasionally; sexually active but not promiscuous; idealistic; depressed; unsure; recently broke up with a steady boyfriend or girlfriend; recently dropped out of college during his/her senior year or recently graduated and started the career for which he/she was trained; travels alone, usually as a backpacker; somewhat shy; has difficulty saying no to strangers; very other-directed; most likely to be a Roman Catholic or a Jew; received religious instruction as a child; of average appearance. Very seldom encountered among cult recruits are firstborn children, gays, blacks, Hispanics, blue-collar workers, the left-handed, or individuals not between the ages of eighteen and forty.

Is there a personality type that is more prone to religious

conversion than are others? William James spoke of a "self-surrender type" of individual, one who is especially suggestible and more likely to lose his equilibrium and be reduced to a sense of inadequacy.[2] Psychiatrist John P. Kildahl describes those susceptible to conversion as generally less intelligent and more hysterical than other comparable individuals. The prospective convert, he maintains, is "subject to mood swings, excitability, fearfulness." In such a personality, "naïveté and moralism are particularly evident: as is a 'general tendency toward over-responsiveness to the emotional implication of events to the exclusion of [the] rational.' "[3] My own investigations have found converts to be of generally superior intelligence although somewhat emotionally and sexually immature. Also, I have found them twice as likely as the population as a whole to have evidenced serious mental disturbances prior to their conversion.

There is also a stereotypical "cult-convert-producing family"—that is, an easily discerned pattern which is more often present than it is absent among our client families. What stands out is a major communications dysfunction. One or both parents simply do not listen to the counselor, their child, or their spouse during our sessions. If they ask questions, they do not listen to the answers. They are inclined to dominate all conversations with self-pitying recitals of past hurts or with self-justifying tributes to their own accomplishments. There is usually a domineering and self-centered parent and a submissive/supportive spouse. One parent is committed to the need for intervention, while the other is neutral or opposed. (The attention-demanding parent may assume either of these roles.) About a third of the time, one parent is extremely cynical about prospects for amelioration of the problem.

Other common characteristics which I have observed are: there are often acute marital tensions and family dysfunctions having nothing to do with the current, cult-related problem; a noticeable percentage (about 10 percent) are themselves religious fanatics, but committed to a cult, sect, or movement other than their offspring's; the parents who demand the most drastic measures are themselves the most scattered, impulsive, and incapable of seeing beyond the emergency of the moment. About one quarter of my clients insist on seeing me as soon as possible because the problem is "a matter of life or death," but will then refuse offered appointments because they interfere with their social obligations, hairdressers' appointments, or other personal business.

A strikingly large percentage of the fathers are entrepreneurs who have founded and built their own successful businesses. They are usually emotionally remote from their children and have a TV repair attitude toward professional services: "Look, I don't want to know anything about what you do or how you do it. I just want to know how much it will cost me to have my son/daughter straightened out. If I had a broken television set, I wouldn't want to take a course in electronics to find out whether or not the repairman was telling me the truth. I would just want to know if the set could be repaired and what the bottom line would be. And if I don't like the price, I throw away the old set and buy a new one."

These stereotypes are partly statistical averages and partly impressionistic observations. It should be remembered that we have served every conceivable sort of family, ranging from warring divorced parents to pillars of the community to group marriages, and that we have been retained on behalf of every type of individual, ranging from David-and-Ricky-boringly-normal to ax murderers, militant Maoist lesbians, and the self-proclaimed "Angel of Death." Once I know the life history and family dynamics of a cult convert or sect recruit, it is fairly simple to reconstruct a plausible account of how the individual and family came to be where they are. But this is facile and unfair. For many individuals come from similar families, have like parents, are subjected to the same stresses, have equivalent peers, are exposed to equally seductive recruitment techniques, and yet do not join a cult. There is a single explanation which I can offer for why some join and some do not. Some like the product—they enjoy the way it feels to be part of a controlling, manipulative, demanding, and self-abnegating milieu. Most who fit the stereotype do not.

CONVERSION AND CONVERTS

Sudden religious conversion has always been and will continue to be commonplace in our society—although specific groups will come and go. Although religious conversion is apparently sudden at its onset, it is often the result of a long process through which the divided self has dealt with religious realities. The event of conversion is unexpected and seemingly spontaneous. Yet the process of incubation may have been gradual and lengthy. Another fundamental truth of the nature of conversion experiences is that they are seldom as radical as they appear. Very few of the religious converts whom I have interviewed were from nonreligious backgrounds. Only an estimated one in ten describes himself as having been an "atheist" or "without religious background" prior to conversion. Most converts report that they had become disenchanted with or indifferent to their childhood religion. But seldom does the convert move directly from no relationship to religion to total religious commitment. The most common form of conversion is not a change in religious affiliation but a change in attitude toward the religion of one's youth. Religious experience is not the establishment of contact with hitherto unknown sacred power as much as it is the transformation of the quality of this contact.

The message seems clear: those who from childhood have participated in religious rituals in the home as well as at places of worship have a starting point for their religious quests. If the attitudes of awe, devotion, and concern for others are obvious in the behavior of family members and friends, it is likely that such attitudes will be re-created in the lives of the next generation. If one's family is only nominally religious or the quality of their participation in religious ritual suggests attendance at a theater rather than membership in a community united by the worship of God and the fellowship of brethren, it is unlikely that a young adult will interpret his later religious experiences within his parents' sphere of understanding.

Those young adults who feel that the religion of their par-

ents is grim, repressive, and compulsive will undoubtedly rebel against it. They may pass through a period of "negative
formation," a time in which all the prohibitions of the past are
violated. But such violation frequently proves as obsessive as
the attitudes against which they protest. Tremendous stress,
dread, and anxiety are involved in the breaking of taboos.
Some of the most dedicated disciples of religious cults and a
disproportionate share of cult leadership are drawn from the
ranks of those who stand in rebellion against a highly structured, morally demanding religious upbringing. Strict conformity—even when it is forced upon the individual—is seldom replaced by lethargy. The children of moral and religious
zealots often become moral and religious zealots. But the convert's morality and religion and those of his parents may be
poles apart. The son of a tent evangelist may become an arch-
bishop of the Children of God; the daughter of Mennonites
may become a Moonie fund raiser.

But what of the children of religiously neutral and ethically
permissive parents? Are they immune to the appeal of the
cults? Certainly not. For every child of strict, conservative parents who finds his or her way into an authoritarian cult, there
are at least ten children from liberal, tolerant families. The
child of parents with clear commitments has something
against which to react, attitudes to reject or refine, and a haven
to which he may return if all else fails. "Live and let live"
provides no sense of direction. How can anyone find a fixed
point of reference in a stress-filled world by reacting to such an
attitude as that reflected in the often heard parental cop-out:
"I don't believe in forcing my children to do anything they
don't want to. I think they should have the right to think for
themselves, to decide on their own values and beliefs. I think
that when they are adults they can choose their own religion."
If only parents who feel this way would realize that they are
telling their children: "I really don't care what you believe or
how you choose to behave as long as you don't hurt yourself or
embarrass me. I just make out the best I can from day to day. I
don't know what I believe, so how can I encourage you to
follow in my steps?" How much better it would be if we admit-

ted our own lack of faith to our children instead of patting ourselves on the back for our superiority to those who compel their children to conform to parental standards of faith and practice.

ADVICE TO PARENTS

I am frequently asked by parents how they can "cult-proof" their sons and daughters. I tell them that the best defense is the creation of an atmosphere of free and open communication. Most of my subjects feel that they were never able to discuss their deepest feelings with anyone—family, friends, or professionals. They report a wall of reticence, busyness, and impatience which stood between them and their parents during their adolescence and college years. The willingness of the instant family provided by the cult or sect to listen sympathetically was for many subjects their first experience of unconditional emotional support. Or so it seemed.

Cult-proofing a child requires a deepening of interpersonal intimacy, the willingness to listen, and more. When I taught college classes during the sixties and seventies, I was often thanked by my students for encouraging them "to think for themselves." I wondered for whom they had been thinking during the previous twenty years. Being autonomous is an art which requires constant practice and much support. Keeping the next generation of children out of authoritarian groups requires that we carefully and cleverly explain to them the dynamics of obedience to authority and conformity. We need simple techniques for illustrating how everyday decisions are influenced by peers, advertising, parental expectations, and one's own insecurities. We need to praise independence and responsibility in decision making. The real villain is gullibility —the inability to examine our actions critically and the unwillingness to say no.

Cults have little fascination or power of attraction for those who know who they are, what they believe, how to think for themselves, and where their lives are going. Parents can do a great deal to encourage the development of a sense of identity, to foster a positive self-image, and to provide an island of unconditional acceptance in the midst of a lonely and threatening world. Parents can and should articulate ethical values and religious beliefs. None of these actions can guarantee that one's offspring will be happy, successful, or cult-free. But not doing them is a prescription for disaster.

ADVICE TO EDUCATORS

High school teachers are especially concerned about the hazards which their charges will confront in the days ahead. Freedom Counseling Center is contacted daily by educators who want to protect the young from unscrupulous recruitment techniques. I have often provided lists of recommended books, articles, films, and videotapes. And the Center has furnished speakers for many classes and assemblies. I have found senior high school students a receptive and curious audience. Younger students scarcely know anything about the world around them, let alone about the dangers of extremism. I am careful to avoid "anticult indoctrination"—e.g., spreading atrocity stories about brainwashing and encouraging vigilante responses. There are numerous ex-cultists conducting high school assembly programs along these lines. It is a pity that the only exposure which many high school students have to religion is through such programs. Scare tactics and the dissemination of "information" about cults remind me of the lamentable outcome of most drug education projects. The potential user does not believe the data or the arguments, and his curiosity is stimulated. I think a much sounder approach is strengthening self-image, enhancing the ability to communicate feelings and needs, and emphasizing the importance of accepting responsibility for one's own decisions. I believe that the Asch and Milgram experiments mentioned above should be adapted for inclusion in the curriculum of every high school in the country. Conformity and unquestioning obedience to authority are the heart of the matter—not anticult indoctrination. And I also think that careful consideration of the history and significance of religion in our society should not be neglected.

ADVICE TO CLERGY, POLICE, LEGISLATORS, AND OTHERS

Fanaticism is ugly—but is seldom maintained for more than a few years. Treating a group like a social pariah has a way of producing objectionable behavior. I for one am totally opposed to banning cults and sects from local and national councils of churches. There is no more effective way of eliciting social responsibility than treating an innovative group like a member of the family of acceptable religions and then communicating objections and reservations to the newcomer on a peer-to-peer basis. Like most of us, the cultist will strenuously defend himself and his group when criticized, and then quietly go about his business in a way that moderates the pattern of behavior which caused the criticism in the first place.

Most of the converts served by Freedom Counseling Center have church backgrounds. They remember the faith of their childhood as uninspiring, undemanding (or overly restrictive), and boring. As a former Congregational pastor, I ask myself: "Where do the churches go wrong?" Perhaps we clergy are too understanding and too reassuring. There seems to be little middle ground in the churches of America between angry, judgmental authoritarianism and wishy-washy, unconditional permissiveness. There is a hunger in the land for moral exemplars, spiritual guides, and social leaders. There is a majority far larger than the "Moral Majority" which is mute at present. Without a faith that is reasonable and spiritually fulfilling, the alternatives are a secularism mired in cynical despair and the confident delusions of the cults.

And while I am a proponent of enforcement of the law and

speedy trials for lawbreakers, I am uncomfortable with the lynch-mob mentality which some would encourage with respect to nonconformist sects. We are a nation of laws—not personal preferences. Religion provides no exemption from the obligation to keep the law. And calling a group a cult does not annul its rights and protections.

We would reassert our contention that unless the state preserves the right to life, which is frequently threatened by fanatic groups, it abdicates its first and greatest responsibility. It is time for the religious exemption clauses to be stricken from all child abuse statutes. And it is time for existing laws regarding hours and wages, worker's compensation, zoning, fraud, birth and death registration, child snatching, theft, immigration, taxes, and practicing medicine without a license to be stringently enforced.

I know that fanaticism can be dangerous to the well-being of the individual, unsettling to the status quo, and distressing to parents whose offspring are caught up in it. I can probably tell more sad cult-related stories than anyone. The fanatic group is probably the greatest instrument for human mischief, self-deceit, and disappointment that has ever been conceived. It is also the most powerful means of overcoming boredom and loneliness, for releasing pent-up energies, and for giving a sense of purpose and identity that any of us will likely encounter. On a one-to-one basis, the fanatic is the most frustrating and annoying creature imaginable. Again, I can tell stories by the week. But the fanatic is a human being who feels what I feel, hurts as I hurt, bleeds as I bleed, and is inevitably forced to come to grips with the same realities as any other human being. However strongly I may disagree with his values and lifestyle, the fanatic is my neighbor and my brother. I will continue to refuse to tolerate his behavior. With love, patience, and good humor, I will seek to persuade him to moderate his irrationality. But I will not deny him the respect which he deserves as my fellow citizen and my companion in the prayer that God's will be done.

Notes

PREFACE

1. David G. Bromley and Anson D. Shupe, Jr., *Strange Gods: The Great American Cult Scare* (Boston: Beacon Press, 1981), p. 1.

CHAPTER 2

1. Rudolf Otto, *The Idea of the Holy*, translated by J. W. Harvey (London: Oxford University Press, 1950).

2. Joachim Wach, *Types of Religious Experience, Christian and Non-Christian* (Chicago: University of Chicago Press, 1951), pp. 32–33.

3. Max Weber, *The Theory of Social and Economic Organization*, translated by A. M. Henderson and Talcott Parsons (New York: Oxford University Press, 1947), pp. 358–59.

4. *The Cults Are Coming!* (Nashville: Abingdon, 1978), p. 117.

CHAPTER 4

1. *The Times* (San Mateo, Calif.), September 24, 1983, p. 6 (Associated Press).

2. Ibid.

3. George Gallup, Jr., and David Poling, *The Search for America's Faith* (Nashville: Abingdon, 1980), p. 47. See also, the Christianity Today Gallup Poll, *Christianity Today*, December 21, 1979 and "How 60,000 Women Feel About Religion and Morality," *McCall's*, May 1978, pp. 127 ff.

4. Ibid., appendix, final page (unnumbered).

5. The documentation for the following statistical data may be found in *Religion and the New Majority* by Gerald S. Strober and the present author (New York: Association Press, 1972), pp. 125–59.

6. Charles Y. Glock and Rodney Stark, *American Piety: The Nature of Religious Commitment*, Vol. I: *Patterns of Religious Commitment* (Berkeley and Los Angeles: University of California Press, 1968), p. 104.

7. Will Herberg, *Protestant—Catholic—Jew* (Garden City, N.Y.: Anchor, 1960), p. 74.

8. Ibid., p. 80.

9. "The Moon and Middle America," *Time*, August 1, 1969, pp. 10–11.

10. Herberg, op. cit., pp. 78–79.

11. Robin M. Williams, Jr., *American Society: A Sociological Interpretation* (New York: Knopf, 1961), p. 417.

12. Joel Kotkin, "What's the Matter with Young People?" *Human Behavior*, May 1977, p. 57.

13. Ibid.

14. Joseph Bell, quoted in ibid.

15. See the present author, *The Gospel Time Bomb* (Buffalo, New York: Prometheus Books, 1984).

CHAPTER 5

1. Michael D. Langone, "On Dialogue Between the Two Tribes of Cultic Researchers," *American Family Foundation Cultic Studies Newsletter*, Vol. II, No. 1 (March 1983), pp. 13–14 (adapted).

2. Alan W. Scheflin and Edward M. Opton, Jr., *The Mind Manipulators* (New York: Paddington Press, 1978), p. 480.

3. Patricia Carrington, *Freedom in Meditation* (Garden City, N.Y.: Anchor, 1977), pp. 261–62.

4. Leon Festinger, *A Theory of Cognitive Dissonance* (Stanford, Calif.: Stanford University Press, 1957).

5. Solomon Asch, "Opinions and Social Pressure," *Scientific American*, Vol. 193, No. 5 (November 1955), pp. 31–35.

6. Stanley Milgram, *Obedience to Authority: An Experimental View* (New York: Harper & Row, 1974).

7. Ibid., p. 189.

CHAPTER 6

1. San Francisco *Chronicle*, September 20, 1983, p. 22 (United Press).

2. San Francisco *Chronicle*, September 23, 1983, p. 33 (Associated Press).

3. *The Times* (San Mateo, Calif.), September 19, 1983, pp. 1 and 10 (Associated Press).

4. Philadelphia *Inquirer*, May 10, 1983, reprinted in *The Advisor*, Vol. V, No. 4 (August–September 1983), p. 3.

5. Ibid.

6. Ibid.

7. *San Gabriel Valley Tribune* (Calif.), September 30, 1982 (Associated Press).

8. Washington *Post,* October 18, 1982, p. A23.

9. Washington *Post,* August 3, 1983 (Associated Press).

10. Chicago *Tribune,* July 9, 1983, reprinted in *The Advisor,* Vol. V, No. 4 (August–September 1983), p. 3.

11. Chicago *Tribune,* December 2, 1982.

12. *Arkansas Democrat* (Little Rock), June 23, 1983, p. 3B.

13. Chet Flippo, "Siege of the Alamos," *People Weekly,* June 13, 1983, p. 30.

14. Topeka *State Capitol-Journal,* October 7, 1980 (Associated Press).

15. *Time,* November 15, 1982, p. 77.

16. New York *Times,* November 4, 1982.

17. *The News-Sentinel* (Fort Wayne, Ind.), May 2, 1983. See also Associated Press reports, May 3, 1983.

18. *Globe,* June 7, 1983, p. 7; Associated Press, November 24, 1982.

19. *The Advisor,* Vol. V, No. 4 (August–September, 1983), p. 3.

20. Ibid.

21. Ibid.

22. *The Advisor,* Vol. V, No. 3 (June–July 1983), p. 1.

23. Ibid.

24. *The Advisor,* Vol. V, No. 4 (August–September 1983), pp. 1 and 3.

25. Ibid., p. 3.

26. Philadelphia *Inquirer,* May 10, 1983. The "religious immunity" provision is found in the juvenile or criminal codes of most states. Illinois, Connecticut, and Washington mention only Christian Science in their laws. Several other states have adopted wording which could only apply to Christian Science—i.e., exempting those who follow the "tenets" of a "well-recognized church" which offers "treatment" by a "duly accredited practitioner." It is incredible to me that such statutes escape the scrutiny of civil libertarians. These laws clearly constitute an "establishment" of religion. Ten years ago, California courts convicted of manslaughter parents who withheld insulin from their son on the basis of their religious beliefs. However, under California's exemption clause, it is legal for Christian Scientist parents to deny medical attention on the same grounds.

27. Ibid.

28. Barbara Grizutti Harrison, *Visions of Glory: A History and a Mem-*

ory of Jehovah's Witnesses (New York: Simon & Schuster, Touchstone, 1978) pp. 97–98.

29. Ibid.

30. I. H. Rubenstein, *Law on Cults* (Chicago: The Ordain Press, 1948 [reprinted 1981]), p. 107.

31. Ibid., p. 44.

32. *First Church Christ Scientist*, 205 Penn. 543, 550–51, 55, Atl. 536 (1903). See also *State* v. *Probst*, 165 Minn. 361, 206 N.W. 642 (1925).

CHAPTER 7

1. See Paul Tillich, *The Dynamics of Faith* (New York: Harper Torchbooks, 1958), p. 8.

2. Eric Hoffer, *The True Believer* (New York: Harper & Row, Perennial Library, 1966) p. 140.

3. Condensed from Thomas F. O'Dea, *The Sociology of Religion* (Englewood Cliffs, N.J.: Prentice-Hall, 1966), pp. 14–15.

4. This discussion of rumors is based upon *Rumor and Gossip: The Social Psychology of Hearsay* by psychologist Ralph L. Rosnow and sociologist Gary Alan Fine (New York: Elsevier, 1976).

5. George Katona, "The Relationship between Psychology and Economics," in *Psychology: A Study of a Science,* edited by S. Koch, Vol. III (New York: McGraw-Hill, 1959), p. 660.

6. Percy H. Tannenbaum, "The Congruity Principle Revisited: Studies in the Reduction, Induction, and Generalization of Persuasion," in *Advances in Experimental Social Psychology,* edited by L. Berkowitz, Vol. III (New York: Academic Press, 1967).

CHAPTER 9

1. "George Gallup Polls America on Religion," *Christianity Today* December 21, 1979, pp.10–19.

CHAPTER 10

1. Robert DiVeroli, "Sociologist Says Cult Growing," San Diego *Tribune,* November 21, 1981, reprinted in *The Advisor,* Vol. IV, No. 1 (February–March 1982), p. 1.

2. Ibid.

3. Alan W. Scheflin and Edward M. Opton, Jr., *The Mind Manipulators* (New York: Paddington Press, 1978), p. 60.

4. Ibid.

5. The transcript of the trial of Patty Hearst (San Francisco, 1976), p. 257.

6. Robert Jay Lifton, *Thought Reform and the Psychology of Totalism,* (New York: Norton, 1969), p. 4.

7. "Some Call It Brainwashing," *The New Republic,* March 6, 1976.

8. References to Clark's views and citations are derived from the following sources: John G. Clark, Jr., "Investigating the effects of some religious cults on the health and welfare of their converts," a paper submitted to the Vermont Legislature, 1977; Clark, "Cults," *Journal of the American Medical Association,* 1979, 242, pp. 179–81; Clark, "The Manipulation of Madness," in M. Muller-Kupers & F. Specht (editors), *Neue Jugenreligionen,* Göttingen (Germany), 1979; Clark et al, *Destructive Cult Conversion: Theory, Research, and Treatment* (Boston: American Family Foundation, Center on Destructive Cultism, 1981), and various transcripts and reports of Clark's public speechs and court testimony.

9. Several instances of Clark's having testified about a person's mental health or fitness to be a parent without having seen them are adduced in Lee Coleman, M.D., *Psychiatry the Faithbreaker* (Sacramento: printed by Printing Dynamics, 1982).

10. *Snapping: America's Epidemic of Sudden Personality Change* (New York: Delta, 1979).

CHAPTER 11

1. Arthur J. Deikman, *The Observing Self: Mysticism and Psychotherapy* (Boston: Beacon Press, 1982), p. 120.

2. Ibid.

3. Ibid., pp. 121–24.

4. Quoted by William Bartley III, in *Werner Erhard,* (New York: Clarkson N. Potter, Inc., 1978) p. 82.

5. Deikman, op. cit., p. 125.

6. Stanley Milgram, *Obedience to Authority: An Experimental View* (New York: Harper & Row, 1974), p. 114.

7. Ibid., p. 115.

8. Ibid.

9. Ibid., pp. 120–21.

10. Ibid., p. 164.

CHAPTER 12

1. Eliana Gil, *The California Child Abuse Reporting Law* (Sacramento: State of California, Office of Child Abuse Prevention, 1983), p. 2. In 1981, 108,930 cases of child abuse were reported in California. Physical abuse accounted for 26.2 percent of the cases; intentional depriva-

tion for 5.2 percent; and sexual abuse for 9.1 percent. Since California has about one tenth of our national population, multiplying the California statistics by ten should convey the magnitude of the problem nationally. In fact, the National Study on Child Neglect and Abuse Reporting stated that during 1981 there were 850,980 official reports of child maltreatment in the United States. Also, it should be noted that the figures record *reported* instances only.

2. William James, *The Varieties of Religious Experience* (New York: New American Library, 1958), pp. 191–94.

3. John P. Kildahl, "The Personalities of Sudden Religious Converts," *Pastoral Psychology,* September 1966, pp. 40–42.

ABOUT THE AUTHOR

Lowell D. Streiker is the founder and Executive Director of Freedom Counseling Center in Burlingame, California. He lives in Foster City, California, a suburb of San Francisco, with his wife Connie and their two dogs.

He holds a bachelor's degree in philosophy from Temple University and an M.A. and Ph.D. in religion from Princeton University. After teaching religion at Temple University for eight years, he served as a member of the national campaign staff of United States Senator Henry M. ("Scoop") Jackson. In addition, he was co-producer and moderator of the television series "Counterpoint" on WCAU-TV (CBS) in Philadelphia. From 1976 to 1979, he was Executive Director of the Mental Health Association of San Mateo County, California. Previously, he was Executive Director of the Mental Health Association of Delaware. In Delaware, he assisted in the rewriting of mental health statutes and spearheaded efforts for the renovation or closing of inhumane treatment facilities.

He is the author, co-author, and editor of ten books. His articles, drama criticism, book reviews, and poetry have appeared in many periodicals.

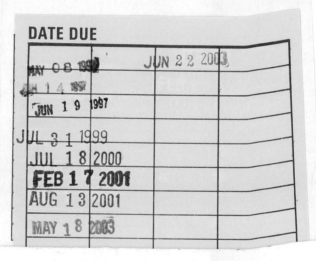